EXPLORING
THE PSALMS

EXPLORING THE PSALMS

by

Erik Routley

THE WESTMINSTER PRESS/PHILADELPHIA

PUBLISHED BY THE WESTMINSTER PRESS®
PHILADELPHIA, PENNSYLVANIA

PRINTED IN THE UNITED STATES OF AMERICA

Library of Congress Cataloging in Publication Data

Routley, Erik.
  Exploring the Psalms.

  "The thirteen chapters of this study were originally written for Crossroads . . ."
  Includes index.
  1. Bible. O. T. Psalms—Criticism, interpretation, etc. I. Title
BS1430.2.R68   223'.2'066   74-20674
ISBN 0-664-24999-X

CONTENTS

Preface   9

Introduction
  The Leading Thoughts of the Psalmists   11

1. Suffering
   Psalms 22, 40, 54, 69   45

2. Victory
   Psalms 139, 113 to 118   52

3. Covenant
   Psalms 81, 111, 57, 50, 44, 16   61

4. Praise
   Psalms 33, 66, 146, 30, 32, 103   71

5. Pilgrimage
   Psalms 84, 42, 43, 120 to 134, 132   81

6. Royalty
   Psalms 98, 93, 96, 97, 99, 100, 72, 144, 101   91

7. Nature
   Psalms 104, 29, 147, 148, 65, 67   101

8. Care
   Psalms 47, 24b, 8, 2, 110, 27, 23   109

9. The City
   Psalms 87, 48, 46, 68, 145, 150   119

10. Faith
   Psalms 95, 82, 19, 119, 90, 91, 77   128

11. Life's Stress
   Psalms 11, 55, 62, 141, 4, 13, 137, 80   137

12. Wisdom
   Psalms 73, 37, 39, 49, 107   146

13. Character
   Psalms 1, 24a, 26, 15, 112, 143, 51   154

Epilogue
   On Using the Psalms in Worship   165

Index of Psalms   171

PREFACE

The purpose of this study is not to provide a detailed commentary, but rather to introduce a reader to the psalms as a basis for his devotions and as a door through which he will come to a special kind of understanding of the Old Testament and of our Lord's teaching.

There are some who feel, as I have heard one such say, "If we understood what the psalms meant, we shouldn't want to sing them." That is an opinion I don't hold myself, except if it is taken quite literally. No, we don't want to sing exactly what the psalmist had in his mind: we can't, since we are Christians. But there is such an astonishing prescience about the psalms—there are so many pre-echoes of the New Testament; and there are such penetrating observations and interpretations of human life, that I think the church has been right to accord them a special place in its worship.

Still, we have to admit that only some churches do this in their liturgies. The richness of the Psalter is often denied to congregations either because editors abridge it too drastically or because those who plan worship do not find a place for it. Too often, all that can

be done is communal reading, which is seldom satisfac-
tory. For this reason I have added an Epilogue, "On
Using the Psalms in Worship."

The thirteen chapters of this study were originally
written for *Crossroads*, studies for adults in Christian
Faith and Life, and are reprinted here with permission.
The chapters consist of brief expositions of the psalms,
in which are noted the salient points of each. Anybody
who wants to go into the matter in a scholarly way will
refer to such learned and excellent commentaries as
those of W. O. E. Oesterley (The Macmillan Company,
1955) and Artur Weiser (The Westminster Press, 1962),
both of which I have used in compiling these notes.

I have thought it best to keep to the order in which
these chapters originally appeared: they were associated
with thirteen Sundays from Palm Sunday to Trinity III
(Pentecost IV). The unfolding drama of the church year,
at its climax, helped to draw out the message of the
psalms for Christians, and it seemed to be an advantage
to link them always with the church's worship. Obviously this study can be read at any time, but it might
prove particularly useful in reference to that season.

Not all the psalms are actually commented on. I have
written notes on ninety-three of the one hundred and
fifty psalms in the Psalter, although there are plenty of
references to the others. A Bible at one's elbow will be a
necessary resource for this study.

ERIK ROUTLEY

INTRODUCTION

The Leading Thoughts of the Psalmists

We were born with this book in our very bones. A small book: 150 poems; 150 steps between death and life; 150 mirrors of our rebellions and our loyalties, of our agonies and our resurrections.

—*A. Chouraqui; quoted in* The Psalms:
A New Translation; *The Westminster Press, 1963*

There are many ways of enjoying, using, and studying The Psalms, but the way we shall follow in these pages is that implied in speaking of The Psalms as a mirror of life.

When it comes to historical criticism of The Psalms, we shall here make use only of items that represent the conclusions of a clear majority of scholars. This is no place for following learned disputes, or for offering as certainties matters which are really speculations.

There are some things concerning The Psalms that we cannot even guess at. Among these is the date at which any particular psalm was written, or the name of its author. About other things scholars seem to have reached at least a measure of agreement in their conjectures, such as the meaning of the titles that are prefixed to some of them. For example, it is usually thought that when we see such an expression as "according to Gittith" or "according to Lilies" we are reading a musical direction, perhaps the accepted name of a tune to which the psalm was to be sung. And when we read, "of David" or "of Asaph," we may be seeing a reference to some earlier collection which was drawn on by the editor of the collection we have.

Other interesting and sometimes puzzling words occur in the titles. Over many is the simple designation "A Psalm." It means, simply, "a poem for singing"; and in a sense all the psalms must be that. But those which originally had the word in their titles keep it in this collection. A few psalms have "A Prayer" in their titles (e.g., Ps. 90); it is obviously appropriate, since these are always meditative pieces; but you find that word also at the end of Ps. 72, indicating that perhaps it was only a designation for a "sacred song."

Occasionally the word *Maskil* appears. Strictly this means a "teaching song," although it is not used with any precision in the Psalter. One is reminded of how many of Charles Wesley's hymns were written with a didactic as well as a lyric purpose.

The meaning of *Miktam* in the titles of Ps. 16 and 57 is very obscure. It may possibly be a reference to "atonement" or "penitence," or perhaps a suggestion about a liturgical occasion for which the piece was particularly suitable. *Mizmor* (Ps. 100) seems to refer originally to "memorial," perhaps to the occasion of the burning of the "memorial offering."

Sometimes a psalm title will refer to some historical episode, not infrequently in the life of David, identifiable from the story of David in the books of Samuel. Normally this should be interpreted not as a composition by David but as a poem or meditation written by a later writer on the subject mentioned. (See, for example, Ps. 51.)

But there are certain ways in which it is helpful to view the Psalter from the perspective of the modern hymnal. The comparison, however, is limited. It must be understood that anything like what we know as congregational singing was impossible for the ancient Hebrews. Our hymnody presupposes printing and literacy. Everybody has a book. In the days of the Temple, the congregation could sing only what everybody knew by heart. A number of the psalms have refrains, and it must be obvious that these at times were sung congregationally. It is at least possible that most of the "pilgrim psalms" (Ps. 120 to 134) were well known as sacred folk songs: they are so brief and epigrammatic. Some of them were possibly sung in association with the pilgrimages to Jerusalem which were part of the religious duty of a faithful Israelite. My own small book *Ascent to the Cross* (Abingdon Press, 1962) assumes and develops that thought.

But on the whole the psalms were heard rather than sung by the congregation. It was a precentor or a choir that would have sung them. Not all would have been used in public worship, for the subject matter of some was inappropriate for communal praise. Others were associated with great festivals of Israelite religion and became traditional and, as we shall see, were well known to our Lord. (See exposition on Ps. 42, 43, and 118 below.)

There are certain other attributes of a hymnal which we can ascribe with propriety to the Psalter. Certain English-speaking Protestants, now regarded as rather old-fashioned, were accustomed to *read* their hymnals at home as regularly as they used them for singing in church. Their hymnal was, as John Wesley said in his famous preface of 1779, "a little body of experimental and practical divinity . . . large enough to contain all the important truths of our most holy religion, whether speculative or practical . . . [yet] not so large as to be either cumbersome, or expensive."

That very well describes the Psalter. Without doubt it is a handy collection of religious teaching, lyrically expressed. Because of its popular style it is brought very close to the consciousness of that ordinary, unprofessional believer to whom, even in those days, many parts of the Old Testament no doubt appeared remote and specialized.

If the Psalter is in some sense a hymnal, one may expect what in fact one finds—that it is the end product of a series of editions. Unlike modern hymnals, it is definitive; after a certain point it was never altered. But before that point it is probable that there were many collections of psalms made at different times and in different places. Somebody, or some group, at some time decided that this collection of one hundred and fifty represented the best that could be found in the existing sources. It is as likely with them as it would be with us that they added a few which had never appeared before.

It is perhaps too much to say that those psalms which have no titles are the latest ones added: this would mean that no fewer than thirty-four were new. But the First Psalm is agreed to be a very late addition, a sort of preface to the new book.

Can anything be inferred from the contents of The Psalms about the editorial processes that formed the collection? Compared with a modern hymnal—very little. There are no dates, no authors' names, and no clear arrangement of the contents of the kind we should expect. But at least we do find that the Psalter is divided into five books. There are lines at four places which read to the general effect "This is the end of the book." Such a line is to be found at the end of Ps. 72. There are lines also after Ps. 41, 89, and 106. This turns out to be less helpful than one might at first expect. Indeed, I myself doubt whether it means more than that that particular psalm stood at the end of the collection from which it came, and that the final line was religiously transcribed in the final edition. This suggestion receives some support by the fact that no such line appears after Ps. 150, which indeed marks the end of this book, but which, we suppose, was not at the end of the collection from which it came.

There is no tabulation of contents such as we find in most modern hymnals—praise here, penitence there, churchmanship elsewhere, and so forth. We do occasionally find a short series of psalms grouped together because they have a similar subject or form. The "enthronement psalms," Ps. 96 to 100, is one such series (but Ps. 93 should be with them): these were all needed at the same act of worship. The "Great Hallel," Ps. 113

to 118 (dealt with in Chapter 2), is clearly another such group. The pilgrim psalms, Ps. 120 to 134 (dealt with in Chapter 5), are clearly a subcollection in themselves, and the book very appropriately ends with five psalms all beginning and ending with "Hallelujah" or "Praise the Lord!"—though they are very different from one another in their content.

The idea of classifying hymns, or psalms, according to content is a modern one. That is why in the ensuing chapters we select psalms from one end of the collection to the other. The ancient editors did not approach them with this kind of consideration in mind. After all, nobody, except the precentor, needed a copy of the whole book, and he knew where to find what was needed. So would a preacher who used them for exposition.

Still, we can suppose that, in some form, the psalms were designed for singing. It would be pleasant if we could indicate in any way to what kind of music they were sung—but all trace of this has been lost. There is a respectable conjecture that Christian plainsong in its most elementary and primitive forms developed from the music of the synagogue—but it is no more than that. But where did the earliest Christian music come from if not from the synagogue? Instruments were certainly used. Occasionally they are actually prescribed in the titles, and Ps. 150 clearly refers to instruments. The expression *Selah*, to be found here and there, is thought to indicate a pause for an instrumental interlude.

But all this is secondary to the theme which it is proper for Christians to pursue. That theme is the content of the psalms themselves, their relevance, their teaching, and their influence on Christian thought. That is what most concerns us, and we shall try in a brief and introductory way to pursue these interests in the chapters that follow.

Our studies will deal with about two thirds of the contents of the Psalter, and they are designed to follow one climactic quarter of the church's year. It is my hope that these studies, together with this Introduction, will help the reader to find his way about the Psalter and to apply the principles of investigation and exegesis that we employ to other psalms not mentioned here.

Therefore it may be helpful briefly to recapitulate the leading themes with which the psalms deal. Other books will take the reader much farther if he wishes to go into it more thoroughly. I rely here on what we gather from such sources as Charles A. Briggs's volume in the International Critical Commentary (1907), and the commentaries of W. O. E. Oesterley and Artur Weiser, mentioned above. In such places as these the reader can find out what he wants to know about Hebrew poetry, meter, lyric forms, and detailed critical points. But for a beginning, these are the chief themes one will encounter if he reads the psalms at all.

Naturally, the overarching theme is God himself. The most precious achievement and highest duty of the Hebrew people was the worship of God. This gave their nation its identity and purpose. No other people was granted so deep and colorful a consciousness of his nature and being.

> O come, let us worship and bow down,
>   let us kneel before the LORD, our Maker!

> For he is our God,
>> and we are the people of his pasture,
>> and the sheep of his hand.
>>> (Ps. 95:6–7)

That is the base upon which the whole religious structure is built.

> Before the mountains were brought forth,
>> or ever thou hadst formed the earth
>>> and the world,
>> from everlasting to everlasting thou art God.
>>> (Ps. 90:2)

The affirmation is as eloquent in English as it is in Hebrew. "Thou art God." The whole of that great psalm has the depth and gravity of a movement of Beethoven. Before, beneath and beyond everything—the being of God.

Yet God has made his nature visible in Creation. The first things the first man saw, according to Old Testament belief, were the solid and substantial objects which God had placed around him, and the mysterious depths of space above him: a creation full of strange adventures.

> The heavens are telling the glory of God;
>> and the firmament proclaims his handiwork.
>>> (Ps. 19:1)

> Thou art clothed with honor and majesty,
>> who coverest thyself with light
>>> as with a garment.
>>> (Ps. 104:1–2)

So it is proper to celebrate in song the earth's fruitfulness:

> The meadows clothe themselves with flocks,
>   the valleys deck themselves with grain,
>   they shout and sing together for joy.
>
>   (Ps. 65:13)

—its teeming animal population:

> The high mountains are for the wild goats;
>   the rocks are a refuge for the badgers.
>
>   (Ps. 104:18)

—the grace and severity of the seasons:

> He gives snow like wool;
>   he scatters hoarfrost like ashes.
> He casts forth his ice like morsels;
>   who can stand before his cold?
>
>   (Ps. 147:16–17)

In thus celebrating the creation, man can call on it to join in the praise of God (Ps. 148), or can see its more terrifying manifestations, such as volcanoes and earthquakes (Ps. 29), as indications of the limitless power of God.

But the God who made all this has a special interest in mankind. It is we who have received special honor, and we who have especially provoked God's impatience.

> When I look at thy heavens, the work
>   of thy fingers,
>   the moon and the stars which thou
>   hast established;
> what is man that thou art mindful of him,
>   and the son of man that thou dost care for him?
> Yet thou hast made him little less than God,
>   and dost crown him with glory and honor.
>
>   (Ps. 8:3–5)

Man is strangely strong, yet strangely weak.

> As a father pities his children,
>   so the LORD pities those who fear him.
> For he knows our frame;
>   he remembers that we are dust.
>   (Ps. 103:13–14)

God's special care for men and women takes the form of
a special relationship set up between them and him—
called "covenant." It is like a conversation, a relationship between grown-up people, in which mankind is
treated as worthy of God's full confidence. When this is
offered to so wayward a people, the psalmist is moved to
an awestruck outburst:

> He sent redemption to his people;
>   he has commanded his covenant for ever.
> Holy and terrible is his name!
>   (Ps. 111:9)

In the face of such mercy, man's response has been
niggardly; in some cases even downright wicked.

> The fool says in his heart,
>   "There is no God."
>   (Ps. 14:1; Ps. 53:1)

> Help, LORD; for there is no longer
>   any that is godly;
> for the faithful have vanished
>   from among the sons of men.
>   (Ps. 12:1)

Moreover, the attraction of false gods is not lost on the
self-indulgent and self-seeking.

> For not from the east or from the west
>   and not from the wilderness comes lifting up;

> but it is God who executes judgment,
>> putting down one and lifting up another.
>> (Ps. 75:6–7)

Naturally—almost childishly—Israel boasts in the honor
of being the one nation that worships the true God:

> Our God is in the heavens;
>> he does whatever he pleases.
> Their idols are silver and gold,
>> the work of men's hands.
> They have mouths, but do not speak;
>> eyes, but do not see.
> They have ears, but do not hear;
>> noses, but do not smell.
>> (Ps. 115:3–6)

> Pour out thy anger on the nations
>> that do not know thee,
> and on the kingdoms
>> that do not call on thy name!
>> (Ps. 79:6)

A civilized modern man would not recognize such
intolerance as a proper attitude toward other religions.
No such thought even entered the mind of an Israelite.
He was proud of his religion, and would have regarded
modesty in that field as blasphemy. We must take him
as we find him, and not without a touch of rueful
penitence at the casual way we often confess our faith
in "God the Father Almighty, maker of heaven and
earth."

One thing that we must notice—lest the psalms lose
all chance of getting their message through to us—is
that the patriotism of the psalmist is always theocratic.

His appreciation of the beauty of his own country, the ground of his affection for it, is always based on his belief that it has been made the special recipient of God's confidence. God has told his people what he has told nobody else; and if this people disappears from the earth, or is brought under the rule of any other people, something irreplaceable will be lost to the world.

This belief is always the ground of the psalmist's passionate appeal to God for protection against his country's enemies. For this reason also the history of his people is so often celebrated in his writings. It was in the things that happened to his people that God made himself and his purposes known—at least to those who would discern the divine word in that history. And broadly, there were four great historic moments, each with a quite different message, to which he refers.

The first and archetypal moment is the exodus. This was to the Jews (it still is) what Easter is to Christians. Indeed, the imagery of the Passover often appears in our own Easter hymns, and historically the events of Easter are intimately bound up with the Passover observance. To the Jew, the exodus was God's supreme intervention in their history: it was God doing the impossible thing—delivering them from Egypt, and making it possible for them to journey back to their homeland.

The exodus story was not only a theophany: it also became an allegory of life's pilgrimage. It must be remembered that the Israelites were in Egypt only because their own country had suffered from famine and had become impossible to live in. The story of Joseph, with all its romance and adventure, is the story of what brought them to Egypt—and indeed of what relief and hospitality they found there. In the course of time this turned into bondage, and the country that had saved their lives became for them a concentration camp. The early chapters of the book of Exodus tell us how impossible it was for them to leave, and how nonetheless they did leave, and all the things they learned on the journey.

It was in the wilderness that they learned to think of themselves no longer as a collection of tribes but as a nation. It was there that they learned, through a series of experiences in which fantastic physical disturbances (quite probably natural and historical) were combined with every kind of spiritual and personal alarm, rebellion, and failure. There are moments in the exodus as exalted as the theophanies of Sinai (when it is actually recorded, almost impossibly, that the elders "saw the God of Israel," Ex., ch. 24), and moments as degraded as the episode of the golden calf. In the end, despite their distrust, their incompetence, and their complete lack of any indication that they deserved it, they came back to their original country. To them, this was how life is lived. They used to remind one another in their liturgies that although they came to have a settled home (and, with certain calamitous interludes, kept it until A.D. 70), they had been a pilgrim people, utterly dependent on divine leadership for their very life.

Of this the psalms continually reminded them. Some psalms rehearse the exodus story at loving length. It is told rather fully in Ps. 78, in Ps. 105–106, and in a different way in Ps. 107. As a spiritual reminder of God's continuing love it is cited in Ps. 77. In their primitive popular song, perhaps one which really did go back to the days of Solomon and even David (II Chron., ch. 5), the story is told in Ps. 136.

Secondly, there was the time of great prosperity and confidence under David and Solomon. After centuries of confused and doubtful hopes, for the first time they became a nation, and indeed a nation highly respected in the eyes of other nations (remember the symbolic tale of Solomon and the Queen of Sheba, I Kings, ch. 10?). This is referred to especially in Ps. 132, but the events that led to it are probably the subject of Ps. 60. The same events are referred to in Ps. 108 and 83, and in parts of Ps. 135 and 136. The assumption was that those days, which lasted only through two reigns, contained promises of a greater age to come. David would yet have a son, a descendant, who would restore Israel's fortunes. Christians know that he did—but not in the manner the psalmists expected.

Thirdly and fourthly (we have to take them together here), there were the great crises of 722 and 586 B.C. The first was the fall of Samaria, in which half of the nation was enslaved by Assyria. Samaria was the capital of the northern half, referred to in the books of Kings as Israel. The southern half, there called Judah (with its capital at Jerusalem), survived. As related in I Kings, the division was the result of the split between Solomon's heirs after his death. Therefore, where a psalm mentions a historic victory, or the preservation of the country from invaders, as in Ps. 124, it may well be to the preservation of Judah that it refers. But there were other crises to which it could equally well refer.

We need have no doubt about the traumatic memories the psalmists kept alive concerning the calamity of 586 B.C. That was when Babylon swept in on Judah, and completed its devastation and political ruin. This was a process which had gone on for more than twenty years since the tragic death of King Josiah in 609. It was completed with the final deportation of many leading citizens, and the destruction of the Temple. For the better part of fifty years they lived in exile in the regions of Babylon, liberated only when in 539 Babylon was in turn conquered by the Persian armies under Cyrus. Isaiah, chs. 40 to 55, deals with this period and the good news of its ending. Jeremiah's memoirs describe the dreadful years just before the final blow fell. Ezekiel's book is the autobiography of a chaplain first to the distressed remnant and then to the exiles.

The most famous reference to this period is in Ps. 137, which unforgettably expresses the grief and despair of the devastated nation that had lost not only its home but, it felt, its God as well. The compensating psalm, which breathes the very spirit of Isa., ch. 40, is Ps. 126: "When we got the news, it was like a dream!" Other references, especially to the destruction of the Temple, are to be found in Ps. 44, 66, and 74. Psalms 85 and 80 contain moving meditations on God's purpose in allowing his chosen people to undergo such degradation and suffering.

Often these references are quite clear. Sometimes, however, we have to say they are doubtful. We have said that there is no possibility of dating the psalms individually; and there were other episodes of victory or defeat to which they may refer. It was the first Temple that was destroyed in 586 B.C. The desecration of the

holy place, in 168 B.C., leading to the revolt of Judas
Maccabaeus, may well provide another point of reference. This event was hardly less traumatic than the
earlier catastrophe, and some of the psalms, in their
final form, may be as late as this. Psalm 74, for example,
is often thought to refer to that later devastation of the
Temple rather than to the earlier one. The message,
however, is the same, whichever of these historic interpretations is right.

A people who had known so much failure and
disappointment, whose period of national success and
prosperity had been so short and ended so calamitously,
must naturally think much of the mystery of God's
purposes. There was among them an inbred tendency to
believe that God had a future for them despite all
appearances. It was this that so eminently brought out
the gift of prophecy in their singers and writers. The
theme of the Son of God, the Anointed, the Messiah,
who would come and revive their fortunes and trample
on his enemies, is referred to especially in Ps. 2 and 110.
These rather savage poems are much quoted in the New
Testament as prophecies of the advent of Christ. But
neither gives any hint of the nature which we were to
see in Jesus when he did come, and neither would be
likely to find a comfortable reception in the Christmas
liturgies of our congregations.

It is appropriate to ask whether any of the psalms as
we have them really were written by David. While we
can be sure that most of them were not—their internal
references preclude that—it is conceivable that one or
two of them were (or are at least founded on) songs
attributed to the king, who was always known to be a

singer. Psalm 18, which appears also as II Sam., ch. 22, was one which was traditionally ascribed to David. Psalm 89 is another of the same kind. Certain others— the most notable being Ps. 51—are ascribed to certain moments in his life but on grounds of style and content almost certainly had nothing to do with him. Psalm 132, which says so much about David with such affection, is attributed, with a certain appropriateness, to Solomon. But the truth is that we can be sure of none of this. Where a psalm is said to be "David's," it is best to take it as some poet's reconstruction of the king's adventures or thoughts. Anybody with imagination could write such a song, as Tennyson wrote the thoughts of Ulysses. But that David was indeed the father of psalmody, in the sense of having inspired it and having no doubt produced its first examples, need never be doubted.

There is a good deal in the Psalter about the qualities required in a leader of the nation; and much prayer for the king. Sometimes we hear echoes of the brief and beautiful meditation ascribed to David at the beginning of II Sam., ch. 23. Psalm 101 is a magistrate's prayer for integrity. Psalm 144 is a king's thanksgiving for victory —an unpromising start, maybe, but some fine lines later on:

> May our garners be full,
>   providing all manner of store;
> may our sheep bring forth thousands
>   and ten thousands in our fields . . . !
> Happy the people to whom such blessings fall!
>   Happy the people whose God is the LORD!
>   (Ps. 144:13,15)

Psalm 149 is a war dance of the most primitive and barbaric sort. Psalm 45 is a song for a king's wedding; Ps. 20, 21, 61, and most famously, Ps. 72, contain prayers for a king at his enthronement or in celebration of it.

But the leader for these people was not only their political guide and protector: he was their priest, and in some sense he impersonated God to them. His prosperity was God's prosperity, his victory was the Lord's victory. So the ceremonies at which he was symbolically enthroned—not only for the first time but regularly as part of the pattern of worship—were climactic occasions of celebration. These are remembered in the psalms that open "The LORD is king," such as Ps. 97 and 99 (NEB). The long ascent of the procession toward the throne is pictured in the "ascent" imagery of such psalms as 47 and 68. This imagery chimes cheerfully with the "ascension" imagery of those Christian celebrations which are centered on the universal kingship of Christ. They are all enthronement psalms in the sense of referring to the human king of Israel; but they express exactly what Christians feel about the reign of their Lord.

This brings to its sharpest point the controversy between Christ and his people. The whole point of this book is to show how wise and universal the psalms are, and how much of their teaching Christians welcome. But we are now beginning to see the difference between what Christianity accepts and what it rejects in the thought of the psalms and indeed of the Old Testament. It is always the outer clothing which the Christian faith changes—all that is needed is to distinguish between that and the inner heart of the psalms.

It was a central conviction for the psalmist, and the

faithful son of Israel, that the purpose of God was to be identified with the purpose of his nation. It did not occur to him that God had a similar purpose for any other nation. Israel's purpose was to infect all the other nations with its faith; but it would do this by the only means open to it—by domination. This is what the last chapters of Isaiah say.

> Then you shall see and be radiant,
>   your heart shall thrill and rejoice;
> because the abundance of the sea shall
>   be turned to you,
>   the wealth of the nations shall come to you.
>
> (Isa. 60:5)

All that heroic pageantry of Isaiah, ch. 60, is—on the surface—about the subjugation of other nations to Israel.

> Violence shall no more be heard in your land,
>   devastation or destruction within your borders;
> you shall call your walls Salvation,
>   and your gates Praise.
>
> (Isa. 60:18)

Violence has departed simply because nobody is fighting anymore against Israel. Exactly the same thought is found in Ps. 72:

> May he have dominion from sea to sea,
>   and from the River to the ends of the earth!
> May his foes bow down before him,
>   and his enemies lick the dust!
> May the kings of Tarshish and of the isles
>   render him tribute,
> may the kings of Sheba and Seba bring gifts!
>
> (Ps. 72:8–10)

In consequence of this passionate and optimistic conviction, the psalmist feels justified in inviting God to subdue the enemies of Israel, and of its king, by any possible means.

There is therefore no trace of the transformation which was wrought in this kind of thought by Christ. It is indeed rarely to be found in the Old Testament at all; perhaps (but even here we cannot be certain) it is hinted at in Isa., ch. 53, where a suffering nation becomes the suffering servant of God. Yet even there, what we are told on the surface is nothing more than that, although there is suffering now, there will be vindication later. The nearest point this passage gets to a Christian utterance is where it speaks of the servant upon whose shoulders are laid the sins of the world. But it would not be wise to say that even there Christ's atonement is positively predicted, or that any more is being said than that the suffering is unjust. This is, we repeat, to read the words off the surface. We know, admit, and rejoice in what Christian hindsight has made of them. Yes, indeed, we now know how much more the poet wrote than he knew.

But in the psalms the suffering of a city or a nation is something which the Lord has laid upon it, and which the Lord in due time will requite. If, as some think, Ps. 129 is a lament of the city personified, then that is the thought the psalmist had in mind.

What Christ contradicted was the nationalist exclusiveness of Israel. To him it was blasphemous to think of God as confining his grace to one single nation. It was for all the faithful. Not for all men whatever: there would (in his thought) be some who were left in the darkness when the Bridegroom came. But this would not be because they weren't Jews, but because they had refused to acknowledge the truth in Christ when they saw it. Given that transformation, all the rest of what these psalms say stands firm. There need now be no hatred, but there will be suffering, on the part of the community of the faithful. There will be no reward for being born into some particular national, or even spiritual, aristocracy; but there will be great joy in the lordship of Christ for those who have been persecuted for the sake of righteousness.

Another great theme of the psalmists, which on the surface needs transformation but whose underlying truth is unshakable, is the theme of worship.

Among the Israelites worship was broadly of two kinds and the psalms were used in both. There was the teaching worship of the local synagogue, and the sacrificial worship of the Temple. Synagogue means simply "meeting house" and there were as many synagogues as there were villages. But there was only one Temple, and since Josiah's time (the late seventh century B.C.) sacrifices could only be performed there, and all the faithful were expected to make the annual journey to Jerusalem to witness them.

Their worship was a complete blending of duty and delight, and both elements appear in the psalms. Psalms 26 and 40 contain much about the duty of worship; Ps. 122 celebrates unforgettably its delight. The city of Jerusalem was a place of special pleasure and honor because the Temple was there—Ps. 48 and 122 tell us that. The pride of the Israelite in being part of a nation whose life centered in the Temple is heard in Ps. 87; the pride of the individual is expressed in Ps. 84. Correspondingly, the deep sorrow of a man who is exiled from his country and who cannot get to the Temple is portrayed in Ps. 42–43:

> These things I remember,
>   as I pour out my soul:
> how I went with the throng,
>   and led them in procession to the house of God.
>   (Ps. 42:4)

Praise and thanksgiving come naturally to a man so blessed—as in Ps. 33, 145, and 150. The details of the liturgies, the dances and processions and songs, are all part of the holiday mood of the great feasts in Jerusalem—reflected in Ps. 68 and 118.

All this is easily translatable into terms familiar to Christians. But what about sacrifices—the slaughter of animals? Admittedly, animal sacrifice is foreign and repulsive to Christian sentiment. But there is also abundant evidence that it did not go uncriticized in the Old Testament. Something is said about this later in the notes on Ps. 50 and 51. It will be sufficient here to mention Micah 6:6–8, the most famous passage on the inadequacy of sacrifice in the prophets, and the echo of it in our Lord's own words: "Go and learn what this means, 'I desire mercy, and not sacrifice' " (Matt. 9:13).

Sacrifice without a corresponding inner generosity was as repellent to the best minds in the Old Testament as it was to Christ himself. Two stories about David give the true spirit of sacrifice in its purest form: II Sam. 23:15–17 and II Sam. 24:21–24. And Ps. 50 says very sternly that nobody must offer a sacrifice in the belief that God needs it.

This, however, is not the only point to be made about sacrifice. In the first place, the spirit behind the sacrifice of animals was a generous spirit. In this primitive society animals were roughly the equivalent of currency: they indicated wealth. The sacrificial animal had to be a perfect animal, because to take what you could most easily part with and call that sacrifice was spiritual fraud. Secondly, sacrifice of this kind was socially divisive. He who had many sheep could afford to give one much easier than he who had few. Abuses with this kind of origin became very common. Thirdly, and more importantly, Christians recognize only one sacrifice: that of God himself in Christ in the atonement. This doctrine is worked out fully in the later chapters of Hebrews.

A Christian then reading these passages can observe that sacrificing an animal was the one thing a Hebrew could *do* about his religion. In some sense it was his sacrament. A further observation is that the generous and self-denying spirit imperfectly expressed in ritual sacrifice of animals is authenticated finally in what Christ did for us.

Like any good hymnbook, the Psalter contains a generous selection of songs about the life of faith. I detect in this seven subsections.

a. Songs of personal thanksgiving provide some of the best-loved pages in the psalms, most of which are dealt with in the following chapters. Psalm 30, Ps. 34 (first part), Ps. 36 (second part), Ps. 116, and preeminently Ps. 103 are such songs. The shadow of personal suffering is nearly always discernible.

> I kept my faith, even when I said,
>   "I am greatly afflicted";

> [when] I said in my consternation,
> "Men are all a vain hope."
>> (Ps. 116:10–11)

> He plots mischief while on his bed,
>> he sets himself in a way that is not good;
>> he spurns not evil.
> Thy steadfast love, O LORD, extends to the heavens,
>> thy faithfulness to the clouds.
>>> (Ps. 36:4–5)

But thanksgiving in such psalms as these is the keynote.

b. Songs of trust in God are equally plentiful. Again, trust in God is contrasted with the vanity and deceptiveness of trust in man. Only trust in God can relieve human suffering.

> There are many who say, "O that we
>> might see some good!
>> Lift up the light of thy countenance
>> upon us, O LORD!"
> Thou hast put more joy in my heart
>> than they have when their grain
>> and wine abound.
>>> (Ps. 4:6–7)

Other well-known psalms on this theme are Ps. 16, 27, 62, 86, 91, 121, 123, 125, and the best known of all, Ps. 23. It is indeed in these psalms that the singer faces the thought of death.

c. And in respect to death it must be remembered that the psalmist's faith gave him no doctrine of a life after death. Death for him was a final and inevitable sentence. He knew of nothing beyond death but "Sheol," sometimes mistranslated "hell" in the older

versions. Sheol was the shady realm where departed
spirits went. It was neither pleasant nor painful; there
was in it no thought of judgment or punishment, nor yet
of reward or glory. The departed just disappeared into
this gray and featureless limbo. In the imaginative
man's mind, the consequence could take him in one of
two ways: either "We must live while we can," or
"There is something here that we haven't been told: as
it stands, it's impossible and absurd to think that this
life comes to nothing."

So, on the one hand, we get the elegiac and haunting
beauty of Ps. 39:

> I said, "I will guard my ways,
>   that I may not sin with my tongue;
> I will bridle my mouth,
>   so long as the wicked are in my presence."
> I was dumb and silent,
>   I held my peace to no avail;
> my distress grew worse,
>   my heart became hot within me.
> As I mused, the fire burned;
>   then I spoke with my tongue:
> "LORD, let me know my end,
>   and what is the measure of my days;
>   let me know how fleeting my life is!"
>
> (Ps. 39:1–5)

—and later on:

> "And now, Lord, for what do I wait?
>   My hope is in thee."
>
> (V. 7)

The imminence of death, this says, should lead a man to

consider his ways, to make the best, morally, of what life is left to him.

A more fierce and pessimistic line is found in such places as Ps. 49—which strongly recalls the sad passages about death in Ecclesiastes and Ecclesiasticus:

> Yea, he shall see that even the wise die,
>   the fool and the stupid alike must perish
>   and leave their wealth to others.
>
> .   .   .   .
>
> Man cannot abide in his pomp,
>   he is like the beasts that perish
>
>   (Ps. 49:10, 20)

Alternatively we have a protesting faith, contrary to accepted teaching, that surely the Lord will "not give me up to Sheol, or let thy godly one see the Pit" (Ps. 16:10). Or:

> What profit is there in my death,
>   if I go down to the Pit?
>   (Ps. 30:9)

d. Suffering, we said, is hardly ever absent from the mind of the psalmist. It is the subject that appears more frequently than any other in the psalms. Occasionally illness is the source—as in Ps. 22, 77, and 41. Psalms 22 and 41 are particularly graphic representations of a sick man's terrors. There can be few more abrasive replies to the romantic deathbed scene than this:

> My enemies say of me in malice:
>   "When will he die, and his name perish?"
> And when one comes to see me, he utters empty words,
>   while his heart gathers mischief;

when he goes out, he tells it abroad.
All who hate me whisper together about me;
    they imagine the worst for me.
They say, "A deadly thing has fastened upon him;
    he will not rise again from where he lies."
Even my bosom friend in whom I trusted,
    who ate of my bread, has lifted his heel
        against me.

                    (Ps. 41:5–9)

This is astonishing language, and, one might think, incongruous in worship. No doubt it is. Yet the whole poem is about the way in which the Lord can comfort a man when he has been snared by even such paranoiac reflections as these. They are the words of a man who has recovered, who got rid of his delusions; and they are offered as a crude sort of comfort for any others who find themselves in similar circumstances. On the more profound and dramatic treatment in Ps. 22, see the notes in Chapter 1.

It is a sense of being in a persecuted minority that seems to preoccupy the psalmist most. It is this sense which gives rise to his more violent passages—those, indeed, which modern readers find most difficult. From these psalms come all those protracted denunciations of "enemies."

The reader must remember that the reading of the psalms isn't an activity like singing hymns: it isn't a declaration of his belief. The psalms are works of art, and works of art reflect the tragedy and distortion of life as well as its glory. But it helps, perhaps, to know just why the psalmist sounds so paranoiac so much of the time. The answer lies in his history, and in the way he was taught it and understood it.

From the outside, the pattern is difficult enough. We
have these tribes descended from Abraham, Isaac, and
Jacob, migrating to Egypt in the dark ages; and we
know what happened in Egypt. Released from that
bondage, they are trapped in the desert for forty years.
There they experienced the extent to which life could be
disappointing and daunting. They arrive in the end at
the "promised land," the land of their dreams, only to
find it populated by peoples who have nothing in
common with them. They make it their business to
settle there and take over as much of the land as they
can. Through long generations of bloodshed and insecurity they stake out a place which they claim the right to
call their own, surrounded by hostile cultures: Tyre and
Sidon to the northwest, Syria to the north and north-
east, Assyria farther away to the east; Egypt, already
forming some sort of Arab alliance to the south; and the
traditionally hostile cultures of Moab and Edom to the
southeast.

All these peoples are united in their hatred of Israel,
whom they regard as pestilential intruders. They all
worship deities and observe religious customs which
Israel rejects.

That is the background which generated a restless
and insecure spirit in the people of Israel in those days.
A nation which is persistently given to self-defense and
a deeply held fear of its neighbors is never going to
become united on that account. No nation could have
been more vulnerable to schism and party strife than
this strange people. Add to this an overwhelming
preoccupation with religious issues, then you will expect, and get, a great deal of religious anger, hatred,

and contempt. God is on Israel's side and he sends them into war against his and the nation's enemies. There is, as we saw, a certain crude and rugged courage about the denunciations of idolatry as practiced by "the heathen" in such psalms as 115 and 138. But much more often than not we hear not of "our enemies" but of "my enemies," and it does look as if many of the psalms were written by people who were in dispute with others over internal religious issues—who were having a running fight of the kind which, unhappily, Christian countries are no strangers to.

The best clue to understanding the times is found in the life of Jeremiah, and it is worth reading over his memoirs again just to recapture the feeling of them. Jeremiah was a young and enthusiastic member of a religious family. His father was what we should call the local minister. Jeremiah lived in the days of King Josiah's reforms, which turned many religious customs upside down, a sort of symbolic cleansing of the Temple. These reforms were generated by the discovery in a forgotten corner of the Temple of a scroll which comprises a large part of what we call Deuteronomy. Anybody who has lived through a time of religious upheaval knows how it splits communities and families down the middle. People who were friends are so no longer (Ps. 55, Chapter 11), and situations arise, as in the case of Jeremiah, when a man is torn between his loyalty to his family and his loyalty to his conscience.

Beyond doubt this kind of thing happened not only in Jeremiah's time but in other times as well. Such occasions generate such utterances as these:

> My soul is cast down within me,
> therefore I remember thee

> from the land of Jordan and of Hermon,
>   from Mount Mizar.
> Deep calls to deep
>   at the thunder of thy cataracts;
> all thy waves and thy billows
>   have gone over me.
> [Yet] by day the LORD commands his steadfast love;
>   and at night his song is with me.
>
>   (Ps. 42:6–8)

The speaker is a priest, or a musician, or a church officer, who has been turned out of his place and exiled to the picturesque north (full of waterfalls and whatnot), which is hateful to him because he has been separated from his friends. Naturally he goes on:

> Vindicate me, O God, and defend my cause
>   against an ungodly people.
>
>   (Ps. 43:1)

Such sentiments are found throughout the Psalter:

> O LORD, how many are my foes!
>   Many are rising against me;
> many are saying of me,
>   there is no help for him in God.
>   (Ps. 3:1–2)

> Lead me, O LORD, in thy righteousness
>   because of my enemies;
>   make thy way straight before me.
> For there is no truth in their mouth;
>   their heart is destruction.
>
>   (Ps. 5:8–9)

> Depart from me, all you workers of evil;
>   for the LORD has heard the sound of my weeping.
>   (Ps. 6:8)

If I have requited my friend with evil
  or plundered my enemy without cause,
let the enemy pursue me and overtake me.

(Ps. 7:4–5)

Judge me, O LORD, according to my righteousness
  and according to the integrity that is in me.
O let the evil of the wicked come to an end,
  but establish thou the righteous.

(Ps. 7:8–9)

Turn any two pages of the Psalter and you will find
passages like that. Often they are far from edifying (as
in Ps. 58 and 109, which even those communities that
sing the whole Psalter usually leave out). One has to
keep in mind the extreme difficulties under which a
faithful Israelite had to operate, not only because of
external pressures but also because of internal controversy. If one feels impatience rising and asks why we
should be cumbered in our sacred literature with the
internal disputes of the Hebrews, the answer is that too
often this is the only way in which a religious consciousness develops in sinful mortals. For the sake of his
underlying faith and his occasional inspirations of fer-
vor, we must take the psalmist as we find him.

We do, of course, find the psalmist in other moods. He
sometimes addresses the matter of personal character
and the good life. The First Psalm declares that it is the
man who keeps God's commandments and holds to his
belief who will flourish: especially he who does not "sit
in the seat of scoffers," or give way to self-indulgent
skepticism. Psalm 15 is sufficiently commented on in the
notes, as are Ps. 112 and Ps. 141 (first part). The virtue

of humility is celebrated in the tiny Ps. 131, and the
pleasure of obedience in the first part of Ps. 34.

Obedience, entire self-giving to the "law" of God, is
the subject of Ps. 19 (second part) and Ps. 119. The
"law" was God's self-revelation to the Jews, and these
are really the songs of complete self-commitment to God
in the highest terms the poet could find.

One other matter in which the psalmist shows interest is social justice and the denunciation of political
corruption. He is often concerned to argue out the
vexatious question why the ungodly prosper and the
faithful are frequently losers in the economic rat race.
Psalm 73 is a graphic account of this problem, and Ps.
37, taking a more complacent line, is another. Denunciations of corrupt rulers find violent expression in Ps. 52,
58, and 94. The extolling of God's superiority to all
earthly rulers, and the certainty that they will be
brought to account before him, is the subject of the
dramatic Ps. 82.

I have constantly written of "the psalmist" in the
singular. Naturally this does not mean that all the
psalms are attributable to one author. It should be
sufficiently obvious that the psalms were written at
different times and in different styles; and the reader as
he gets to know them will find affinities between the
styles of some and those of other Old Testament books.
Some read like extracts from the historical books;
others like a comment on prophecy. Some suggest the
comforting message of Isa., chs. 40 to 55, others the
agonies of Jeremiah. Some embody the ethical concerns
of passages like Micah 6:6–8, others the denunciations of
Amos and other minor prophets. It is clear that in this

way as well as in certain others the Psalter is like a
hymnal. If it is called "The Psalms of David," this can be
paralleled by the use of the phrase "Charles Wesley's
Hymns" as a title for an English hymnal of 1876 which
was used by Methodists and which certainly contained
many hymns not by Wesley himself.

That ancient practice, commended in Catholic and
Anglican circles, of reading the Psalter through once a
month (which is provided for in the old offices of matins
and evensong) is still worth encouraging as a framework for private devotion. The old prayer books divide
the Psalter into sixty sections, one for each morning and
evening of thirty days. If you read them in this way,
taking them as they come, you find that occasionally you
have a group of psalms all in the same mood, and at
other times a fascinatingly contrasted series. But in the
end you are left with a complete exploration of the
moods and tides of human faith. And you will be
surprised how often you come across phrases that our
Lord incorporated in his teaching, and ideas that clearly
influenced the way in which he expressed himself, as
reported in the Gospels. And you will find that Ps. 23
and 103, beautiful though they are, are not the only
psalms worth reading.

1. SUFFERING

Psalms 22, 40, 54, 69

The chapters of this study are coordinated with thirteen Sundays in the church year, beginning with Palm Sunday. Our first study, however, takes its theme from Good Friday. Four psalms, each of which deals in its own way with human suffering, have been grouped for our initial exploration. Where better could we begin than with Ps. 22, the psalm most closely associated with the suffering of our Lord?

PSALM 22

Psalm 22 opens with words that the Gospel accounts have made sacred: "My God, my God, why hast thou forsaken me?" But we must first look at it as if we were unaware of that sacred association.

Despite the heading, which suggests that it was adapted at some stage for choral singing, the psalm is essentially an intimate and personal composition. The writer did not originally have in mind the high and holy matter of the crucifixion. He was concerned with bodily sickness.

The psalmist begins (*vs. 1–5*) by complaining of his condition, and contrasting his sense of being deserted by God with the faith that his friends are constantly proclaiming—that God is holy, "enthroned on the praises of Israel." He describes his symptoms in detail (*vs. 6–21*), and dwells on the mental anguish, the nightmares and perverse thoughts, the monsters of his dreams, that accompany his pain. Not only God but all his friends, also, are against him. He cannot share their easy confidence in God.

It reminds one at once of The Book of Job, which equally recalls ordinary human experience. It is not bodily pain that most sears the heart of the man of faith; it is *faith itself* that generates the worst suffering. He had believed, but where is his belief now? If it is the man of faith who suffers more, it is the professional proclaimer of faith who suffers most—the man who is haunted in his hospital bed by the thought: I ought to be doing better than this; or: People will expect me to do better than this. That is where the psalmist stands.

In Ps. 41 there is a parallel passage, in which a sick man's tortured mind represents even his friends and visitors as part of a conspiracy against himself. "They're all waiting for me to die," he says in effect (Ps. 41:5–7). So here, in *Ps. 22*, "a company of evildoers encircle me" (*v. 16*). The evildoing may well be in the sufferer's imagination, but the worst of it all is that he feels not only that God has deserted him but that he has deserted God.

In the end (*vs. 22–31*), his prayer is answered. The scene changes to praise and glory. He can walk again and go about among his friends. Psalms of suffering do not always have a happy ending like this, but this psalm raises two important points which we ought to consider.

The first is that, through his personal thanksgiving to the God who did not desert him and his candid record of his misery, the psalmist is telling us that despair is never final and that a temporary sense of despair is nothing to be ashamed of. We need not believe that those whose faith is most evident never know times when it flickers almost to the vanishing point.

But secondly, when we remember our Lord's saying the first words of this psalm during the crucifixion, we must draw back from interpreting those words as a cry of self-pity. Would not the final verses of the psalm be also in his mind? Did he not, as the gospels record, quote a little later Ps. 31:5, "Into thy hand I commit my spirit"? Surely it was the great hymns of his people's faith that comforted our Lord in his last hour. He was taking to himself all their failures of faith and making of them a victory of faith—his victory—so that he could pray for the evildoers who surrounded him, "Father, forgive, forgive."

PSALM 40

Another psalm for Good Friday is *Ps. 40*. This is less a psalm of sickness than one of generalized suffering. It opens with thanksgiving to the Lord for whom the psalmist waited patiently. We should say, to express the same thought, "waited and waited." In the end the Lord delivered him from "the desolate pit" (one thinks of Joseph, Gen. 37:24, 28). One could hardly look for a more vivid description of the dirt, the quicksand, the clinging

foulness of the world's suffering and sin, than the words
"miry bog," of *v. 2*. When all was over, the Lord "put a
new song in my mouth, a song of praise" (*v. 3*). From
this experience the psalmist learned of the direct
connection between obedience and deliverance (*vs. 6–8*).
What before (*v. 6*) had been formal religion now
becomes living faith: "Lo, I come; . . . I delight to do
thy will." The knots of sorrow were released as soon as
he could relax in obedience, as one falls safely when
relaxed.

He goes on (*vs. 11–17*) to speak of the troubles that lie
ahead, and how he will again need God's delivering
power. The next testing will probably be worse. We
cannot go through life without meeting some people
who will rejoice at our failures, who declare themselves
the enemies of our welfare. No one is ever without the
experience symbolized by the word "enemies" in the
Psalter. For all the psalmist's exalted experience, he is
still "poor and needy" (*v. 17*).

There is a passage in Heb. 10:5–8 that applies this
psalm directly to Christ. From that passage we learn
that it was in his obedience to God that Christ found his
peace and his strength. The gospel of Christ calls us to
that condition of life in which we say, as he said, "I
delight to do thy will."

PSALM 54

It is impossible to think of the cross without thinking
of a battle between the powers of good and the powers
of evil. That is why this brief and violent psalm is
another psalm often used in church liturgies for Good

Friday. It raises one point for our present study, and one only: what to do with the "enemies" so often referred to in the Psalter. The enemies here are nothing spiritual or symbolic; they are real, malignant enemies. The psalmist calls on God to defeat them and to save him. Tradition, indeed, held that David sang this psalm when he was in great danger from the Philistines (I Sam. 23:19), but that may be only a popular and unfounded notion.

Christians, who are commanded to love their enemies in their own lives, understandably wonder what help they can get from psalms like this. There are two ways of applying such Scriptures to life: One is by saying, "Humanly speaking, I am no better than the psalmist, and probably a good deal worse, so I need at least as much as he to turn to God in my trouble." But then you remember the Sermon on the Mount and say, "But I may be mistaken—more is expected of me than this." Further, you recall that our Lord said that when the time of testing really comes, "a man's foes will be those of his own household" (Matt. 10:36). There will never be a time for any of us when there are not enemies—at least within ourselves—which, with God's help, we must fight.

In its opening verse the psalm uses the word "vindicate"; this is a key word for the psalmist. Often, as here, the poet says, in effect, "I've been framed," and calls on God to put the record straight. The Christian revelation shows how God "vindicated" Jesus in the resurrection, proving the falsity of every charge laid against him by his earthly enemies. Pentecost similarly showed us that for the faithful there is an "advocate" in the Holy

Spirit. We can be assured that a prayer such as *Ps. 54* can be answered by God in his own way because of the meaning Good Friday has given to it.

PSALM 69

Finally, we come to a vivid and, in places, truculent psalm whose chief subject is the suffering of a man who is taking a moral stand. Some people have thought it was written by Jeremiah. It could have been, but of course there is no evidence that it was. But its key verse is *v. 9*, "Zeal for thy house has consumed me, and the insults of those who insult thee have fallen on me." That is pure Jeremiah.

But it is also Christ. John's account of the cleansing of the Temple quotes its first line (John 2:17), and Rom. 15:3 quotes its second line as a description of the work of Jesus.

After reading the other psalms of Good Friday, we find this one especially meaningful. Here is a man enduring the mental agony that comes from alienating himself from his friends for a principle. The anguish (which we see expressed without relief in a fifth Good Friday psalm, Ps. 88) issues in terrible words about his adversaries (*vs. 22–28*). He is sorry for himself; he cannot help it. It would all be unedifying, if there were not *v. 19:*

> Thou knowest my reproach,
>   and my shame and my dishonor;
>   my foes are all known to thee.

Even if the "shame" and the "dishonor" are not so much sins being confessed as grievances complained of, the psalmist knows that God knows them all. If he were not sure that God knows, his despair would be too complete for him to be able to sing at all.

And there is faith. That is the beginning of obedience, and obedience is the beginning of godly fear, and the fear of the Lord is the beginning of wisdom. Overarching the whole system of life is the perfection and the justice of God. For all their falling away, for all the distortions that life's violence works in them, the psalmists believe that. And what they reached out for, Christ in his passion brought down from heaven and gave to us all—the secret of obedience, peace, and victory.

2. VICTORY

Psalms 139, 113 to 118

In the ancient liturgies of the church still used today, the first words heard at the Easter Eucharist are these:

> I am risen, and am still with thee, alleluia!
> Thou hast laid thine hand upon me, alleluia!

PSALM 139

Those words are adapted from *Ps. 139*, and although that incomparable lyric of God's presence and compassion hardly needs comment here, it is worth pausing for a moment to observe the light that this Easter association throws on it.

The church is reminding us that, just as Ps. 22 takes us directly to the cross of Christ, so *Ps. 139* becomes a symbol of his whole life and his resurrection.

"Thou hast searched me and known me!" (*v. 1*). Consider how, in the life of Jesus, God did precisely that. There is no area of human life, and human death, that God did not search and know in him. Born at Bethlehem, living at Nazareth with his parents, worshiping with them in synagogue and Temple, walking the streets of Jerusalem and the lanes of Galilee, meeting the learned and the simple, the brave and the weak, the healthy and the sick, the shrewd and the feebleminded—in all these experiences of Jesus, God searched and knew his world. In the suffering and death of Jesus we hear, "Whither shall I flee from thy presence?" In Jesus' recognition of Nathaniel under his fig tree, in his handling of the devices of Judas and Caiaphas, the clumsiness of Peter, and the passions of the Sons of Thunder, we hear:

> Even before a word is on my tongue,
>   lo, O LORD, thou knowest it altogether.
>
> (V. 4)

Then, in the resurrection: "When I awake, I am still with thee" (v. 18).

It is the knowledge that *Ps. 139* has "come true" in the work and triumph of Christ that can really nourish a man's faith. And just as Christ brings Ps. 22 to true life in his suffering, so he cleanses *Ps. 139* of man's imperfections. He injects love where *vs. 19–22* fall into human anger. The psalm is a matchless celebration of the creative power and continuing mercy of God. Easter tells us that the knowledge of this is not for psalmists only, but for all who will have faith.

PSALM 113

And now we turn to six psalms often referred to as the Hallel psalms. "Hallel" means a song of praise to the Lord. Psalms 113 to 118 formed a chain of praise which

was always sung at the Passover, and which our Lord
and his disciples certainly sang at the Last Supper
(Matt. 26:30). Certain of them were sung at other times
as well, but taken together they make a comprehensive
act of praise that tells the story of salvation as Israel
understood it.

Psalm 113 is one of the most attractive and simple of
all the psalms of praise. It calls on the "servants"—that
is, the worshipers—of the Lord to sing praise; and the
worshipers (who in effect are the choristers) call on all
Israel to keep the song of praise always alive, like the
fire on the altar in Lev. 6:13.

God, immortal and eternal, observes and comforts the
afflictions of mortal men (*v. 6*); the farthest distance of
the heavens cannot hide man's need from God. If God
sees a man who is an outcast of society, he comes to his
rescue (*v. 7*). (One is reminded of Job on his ash heaps.)
Those were rough times; sickness and injustice equally
abounded. The man whom God befriends is often in the
psalms the man whom society has treated badly; the
folklore of faith defies the folklore of human society,
which (again as in Job) usually insists that suffering is a
punishment for wrongdoing.

One particular kind of ill fortune caused special
distress in those days—childlessness in a woman. God's
mercy in that situation (archetypally celebrated in the
story of Abraham and Sarah, Gen., ch. 12) is mentioned
in *v. 9*. The same note, but transformed by that turning
upside down of human values which the gospel brings to
every area of life, is heard in the Magnificat—"He has
regarded the *low estate* of his handmaiden" (Luke 1:48;
italics added).

For the Israelite at the Passover Feast the psalm is a reminder that no human misfortune is too great for God's healing, and that no human values are immune from the judgment and reversal that God's visitation may bring at any moment.

PSALM 114

After praise, history. For Israel, the exodus was "Easter": the deliverance from the labor camps of Egypt, the dawning of national responsibility and moral sense, the tremendous experience of God's majesty in the loneliness and terror of the desert. This was the historic hinge on which all faith turned for the people of which our Lord was born. So they sing of what happened "when Israel went forth from Egypt" in a folk song that expresses in simple, vivid language an experience whose inner realities are beyond all expression.

The gospel sends this faith in the infinite power of God crashing into human life. "The mountains skipped like rams," said the old song (v. 4). "Whoever says to this mountain, 'Be taken up and cast into the sea,' and does not doubt in his heart, . . . it will be done for him," said Jesus (Mark 11:23). Only Paul's comment need be added: "If I have all faith, so as to remove mountains, but have not love, I am nothing" (I Cor. 13:2). History underpins faith, faith moves into life, and life in Christ teaches love.

PSALM 115

In *Ps. 115* history teaches its primary lesson. Here the psalmist sings of the moral experience that the exodus story taught. Historic ecstasy gives way to high-spirited, cheerful obedience. It contrasts the privileges of Israel's faith with the lonely unbelief of "the nations" (*v. 2*). In the psalms "the nations" are always the heathen nations. Israel has now found a purpose in living; these oppressed and enslaved people are now committed to leading the world to faith. The central fact that they are destined to proclaim is the fact of the *living* God.

The living God is contrasted, with a high good humor that recalls Isa., chs. 41 and 44, with the dead and profitless gods of the heathen. Israel now believes in a God who moves with them, who observes every detail of life (Ps. 113), who is about their path (Ps. 139). Dead things beget no praise, but the praise of Israel is immortal (*vs. 17–18*).

This may all sound tribal, nationalistic, and repellent to modern liberal notions. That is of no consequence. This is the song of a people with a purpose and a mission. They must learn much yet, but the exodus has taught them how much there is to learn.

PSALM 116

The singer at his Passover meal now turns aside into calmer waters and sings a psalm of pure personal thanksgiving. This is the quiet movement in the symphony formed by these six psalms. The key verse is *v.*

7—"Return, O my soul, to your rest"—that is, *come home to God.*

The whole Passover context is, of course, one of "coming home." That is what the forty years' migration from Egypt to Canaan was, a coming home. The pilgrimage takes a man, as it took the nations, through dangerous and depressing places. He will know "the pangs of Sheol" and the failure of faith in human nature (*v. 11*). But because the Lord has never deserted him, he will give thanks in the presence of all God's people (*vs. 14, 18*). And above all he will take "the cup of salvation" (*v. 13*).

To Christians "the cup" irresistibly suggests the sacramental cup; to Israelites of our Lord's time it suggested the Passover cup. But with the original writer this was not so. It was others who ordained that this should become a Passover psalm. Israel's faith is rooted in dark places, and just here we can see a long way down. It is quite possible that the idea of the "cup" is rooted in a strange passage in Num. 5:18–28. This passage prescribes that a certain situation of dispute shall be decided by "ordeal." The priest is to offer a "cup of bitterness" to the supposed offender; if the drink harms her, her guilt is established; if not, her innocence.

This cup of bitterness (some kind of mild poison, one supposes) is the cup of mystery, the cup of decision. It represents an emergency in which the primitive instinct is to trust only to luck, or to irrational and supernatural forces. In the psalmist's hands, the cup of bitterness becomes the cup of rescue (salvation). Whatever life brings out of its mysterious treasury of bane and blessing, he will drink of the cup of life and be not only

unharmed but *saved*, because before the Lord he is
already justified. Life, to the ordinary believer—Israelite or Christian—is, without God, nothing but an "ordeal." With God is the only release from anxiety,
superstition, insecurity, and guilt. (Rom. 5:1.)

PSALMS 117, 118

After this personal digression, we return to public
worship. In *Ps. 117* there is a burst of praise (which
Isaac Watts made into the hymn "From All That Dwell
Below the Skies"), celebrating the eternal mercies of
God. Then we move into the long, rhythmic, dramatic,
and obviously congregational *Ps. 118*. This was Luther's
favorite psalm—indeed, a psalm for anyone who has
plumbed the depths and scaled the heights.

As we have it, *Ps. 118* is a dramatic song designed for
a procession at worship. First there are four verses of
pure praise, on the lines of that great primitive psalm
with a refrain, Ps. 136 (which no doubt was the psalm
sung at the dedication of Solomon's Temple—II Chron.
5:13). Then there is a long section (*118:5-20*) in which, as
the procession approaches the Temple gate, the king,
who is also the priest, declares his faith. His faith is
Israel's faith; what he says of himself the people are
ready, if they are faithful, to say of themselves. The
king impersonates his people and stands on their behalf
before God. So he tells how God has befriended him and
delivered him and refreshed his faith by discipline and
blessing, by times of terror and times of wealth.

This takes us to *118:21*, by which time the king has
commanded the Temple gates to open, and stands ready

to go in and perform his part in the great sacrificial feast.

What feast? It is almost certainly the Feast of Tabernacles. This is the new year festival, the covenant festival (see Chapter 3) and the harvest festival of Israel. It takes place in the autumn and contains a rehearsal of the historic faith within the context of a dramatic reminiscence of the exodus.

This psalm, then, was one of the really well known hymns of Israel, and it is not surprising that there are at least three highly significant reminiscences of it in the New Testament.

First, there is the blessing given by the assistant priests to the king as he rides into the Temple: "Blessed be he who enters in the name of the LORD!" (*118:26*). This was sung or shouted (and how strange it must have sounded!) by the people who welcomed the King of Israel into Jerusalem on the first day of what we now call Holy Week. (Mark 11:9.) In using those words, the people declared: "This is the King who *really* represents his people. He is the Prince of Peace."

Secondly, there is the song of the rejected stone (*vs. 22–23*), which Jesus used at the end of his parable of the vinedressers (Mark 12:10–11), clinching the message of his parable by quoting the well-known hymn. So often he said, in effect: "This is what you really believe; this is what you are always saying or singing; now it has come true. Do not be afraid to welcome it!"

Thirdly, there is *118:27*, which reads, "The LORD is God, and he has given us light." In John 7:37 Jesus opened one of his greatest discourses "on the last day, the great day," which was indeed this Feast of Tabernacles. Farther on in the same discourse he said, "I am the light of the world" (John 8:12). This cannot be coincidence. This is a memory which the Fourth Evangelist alone preserves (or a tradition for which he alone is responsible). The psalm of light is quoted by him who is the world's light, so that men can now and forever say, "The LORD is God, and he has given us light," and can worship and praise with a faith from which all fear and all uncertainty have been cast out.

3. COVENANT

Psalms 81, 111, 57, 50, 44, 16

The same ancient liturgies that appoint Ps. 139 for Easter Day also propose Ps. 81 for the first Sunday after Easter. This and some kindred psalms which we are about to consider are especially associated with that Feast of Tabernacles, which we mentioned in the previous chapter, and about which we must now say a little more.

The Feast of Tabernacles was just half a year away from that other great exodus festival, the Passover. Of the three parallel emphases in the festival, the oldest was that of the new year, and the harvest was the next oldest. That of the covenant, and the least primitive, was the emphasis that gave it its name—tabernacles, or tents. The historic situation that gave rise to it in the form that our Lord knew is described in Neh., chs. 6 to 8. The people of Israel had, in Nehemiah's time (about 445 B.C.), shown a disastrous tendency to cultivate a false sense of security, to sink into inert complacency. To correct this, we learn from Nehemiah that once a year they would be required to leave their homes, whether or not they lived in Jerusalem, and build themselves "tabernacles"—booths or shacks—either around the city walls or on the flat roofs of their own houses. There they must camp for a few days to remind themselves of the time when their fathers lived like that during the exodus from Egypt.

This is not an emphasis that appears in the psalms associated with the occasion, because most of them had already been written by the time the feast was inaugurated in this form. Nehemiah added this idea of "pilgrimage" to an existing festival, which already had an association with the exodus in that it was the time when the people remembered their unique encounter with God in the covenant of Sinai.

"Covenant," in the religion of Israel, was the word that symbolized the approach of God to his people. It contained a mighty paradox. On the one hand, God was not only infinite and inaccessible but of such purity and glory that a human being might not look upon him and live. (Ex. 33:20.) On the other hand, God had made himself known to his people. (Ex. 24:10.) Since the days of Noah, God had made it clear that his relation with his people would never be that of master and servant, or of potter and clay; it would be a kind of friendship, or conversation, involving trust. On God's side the movement is "mercy" ("steadfast love" in the RSV); on man's side, it is faith. This is the mystery which Israel celebrated at the new year.

PSALM 81

The jubilant and colorful *Ps. 81* works out these ideas with great economy. *Verses 1–4* are a call to corporate

praise. The congregation is summoned by the new moon
and the new year trumpet, to recall how God established
a "statute" for Israel "when he went out over the land
of Egypt." That, precisely, is the covenant of Sinai.

Then Israel speaks: "I hear a voice I had not known"
(*v. 5*). Unsure of their purpose, doubting their future,
Israel heard a voice (at Sinai) saying, "I relieved your
shoulder of the burden" (*v. 6*). The voice never left them.
They heard it in Sinai's thunder, in the trials of the
journey, such as that of Meribah. (Ex. 17:7.) But Israel
was not obedient; especially, Israel had not learned to
trust. (Ex. 16:3.) The rest of the psalm (*vs. 8–16*) recalls
this failure to trust which amounts to a breach of
Israel's side of the covenant. A return to faith (*vs.
13–16*) will bring blessing from God.

It may appear crude and naïve; and indeed it is a
superficial view of "covenant" to say (like Jacob at
Bethel in Gen. 28:20), "If you will do your part, I will do
mine." But that is not the real point of the psalm. What
matters is that, in folk songs like this, Israel constantly
recalled the story of her salvation. In many psalms this
story is written out; see Ps. 78, 105, 106. Sometimes it is
the theme of a shorter psalm, like Ps. 124, or of this one.

PSALM 111

A different approach to the same object is made by
Ps. 111 (one of the "proper psalms" for Easter in the
Anglican Book of Common Prayer). The leading idea
once again is "covenant," but here it is associated not
with the exodus but with a more highly developed
spiritual insight into the ways of God.

It is, indeed, a very different kind of poem from Ps. 81, even in its outward form. It is an acrostic: each new clause begins with a successive letter of the Hebrew alphabet. The effect is to make this, like other psalms employing the same device, a song gathered around one point (variations on a theme, as it were) rather than a continuous passionate utterance. This is the only psalm that uses acrostic by short clauses; Ps. 25, 34, 103, and 145 use it by whole verses; Ps. 37 changes the letter at every second verse; and Ps. 119, the most astonishing of all, begins each verse of each eight-verse section with the same letter, moving down the alphabet as one section succeeds another.

The theme of *Ps. 111* is the working out of God's "covenant" in his relations with men: his "wonderful works" (*v. 4*), his providing food which men of faith recognize as a divine gift (*v. 5*), his protection of the people through history (*v. 6*), his establishment of the moral law (*vs. 7–8*). All of this is "redemption" and "covenant," and the moral of it all is expressed in a phrase reminiscent of Proverbs rather than of the Pentateuch: "The fear of the LORD is the beginning of wisdom" (*v. 10*).

This "fear of the LORD" is that mixture of joy and awe which is the religious man's natural response to the glory of God. It is not a fear to be exorcised—"covenant" has already driven out that kind of fear—but a fear to be cultivated. It is the fear of the lover that he may displease the beloved. Its opposite is a familiarity that generates contempt—expressed precisely in Ps. 10:4:

> In the pride of his countenance the wicked
> does not seek him;

all his thoughts are, "There is no God."

This thought is echoed dramatically in Ps. 53:1:

> The fool says in his heart,
> "There is no God."

PSALM 57

How then, in a perilous world, will a man find assurance? Another Easter psalm, *Ps. 57*, gives part of the answer. Here we are back in the thick of it. The old tradition was that David wrote this psalm when he was hiding at En-gedi from the wrath of Saul (I Sam. 24:4). Whatever one believes in the tranquillity of devotion, what can one believe on the battlefield of life? This particular believer has this faith: "He will send from heaven and save me." Imprecations on enemies alternate with gestures of faith in God, and the root of that faith is the covenant of which in happier times the singer can sing with calmer reflection. The psalm became an Easter psalm because of the idea that in the resurrection God rescued all mankind from death by the rescue of his Son (*vs. 3–5*). The ancient theme, however, is that God's covenant can, when mankind is in need, appear not merely as exhortation but as saving energy.

PSALM 50

Something more about covenant is taught in the Fiftieth Psalm, which deals with true worship. It is of the greatest interest because its teaching seems to be far removed in time from that of such famous texts as

Micah 6:6–8 or Ps. 40:6–8. Advanced minds in the Old
Testament often express impatience with the formali-
ties of worship. Jeremiah, Amos, and Isaiah are full of
denunciations of vain rites; those prophets were fond of
saying that God has no use for sacrifices, which can be
performed faithfully though the worshiper practices
injustice.

That was not the only way to look at it. Progressive
people today often seek to expose hypocrisy by saying
much about the unnecessary waste of money and
manpower that public worship involves, especially when
it is given to large gestures, such as new cathedrals, or
to expensive ones, like some kinds of religious art. But
what *Ps. 50* says must not be ignored. For to the
ordinary man it says that it is quite proper to worship
God in the traditional way, so long as you don't for a
moment entertain the idea that you are doing God a
favor by worshiping. This is the meaning of the para-
doxical passage in *vs. 8–10:*

> I do not reprove you for your sacrifices;
> > your burnt offerings are continually before me.

However,

> > I will accept [as a favor] no bull from
> > > your house,
> > nor he-goat from your folds.
> > For every beast of the forest is mine,
> > > the cattle on a thousand hills.

In other words, offer what you will, but in the spirit
of Luke 17:10: "So you also, when you have done all that
is commanded you, say, 'We are [but] servants . . . .' "

This injunction to offer sacrifice for love's sake, or for duty's sake, but not in a patronizing spirit, is framed between two statements about God's covenant. The first is that the foundation and cause of all human worship is that God has spoken (*vs. 1–6*) in the perfection of beauty. The second is that those who have no idea of duty or love, who encourage wickedness, caring not whom they hurt by word or example, are rejecting the whole idea of covenant (*vs. 16–23*). So in the end it comes to much the same conclusion as the familiar prophetic texts, but by a different route.

PSALM 44

Another idea associated with the covenant festival, hinted at in Ps. 81, discussed earlier, is that of penitence. Now, in *Ps. 44*, we hear the sound of national lamentation. What, after all, does one say on a festival of thanksgiving held in a time of national disaster? One turns in grief to the author of all salvation.

So the singer recalls what the fathers have told their children about the mighty works of God (which means the preservation of the nation in past days). A single singer—originally, no doubt, the king—confesses that he trusts in God and not in his own power (*vs. 4–8*). But then he goes on to tell of catastrophe: of defeat in battle (*v. 10*), of deportation (*v. 11*), of enslavement (*v. 12*), of the giving over of the city to wild beasts of the desert (*v. 19*). The people, bowed in humiliation, appeal to God to rescue them again. Was it because of their disobedience that all of this came upon them? But even in this sorry day they will keep faithful. (*Vs. 20–21.*) Where is the love of God? Will it not show itself? (*Vs. 23–26.*) *Verse 22* forms part of that immortal passage at the end of Rom., ch. 8, the charter of Christian faithfulness under affliction.

Here, while people are singing the praises of the covenanted love of God, one feels the very heart of the Old Testament tragedy. The love of God is indeed veiled, hidden even from the eye of faith at times (cf. Ps. 77:9). In Christ it has been shown with all its mysteries revealed. But it is the faith of men who did not know Christ that is so precious in the psalms.

This psalm, written under stress of grievous national sorrow, may well have become a hymn of communal penitence in later days. It is well to remember the Dunkirks or Corregidors of national history even in times of tranquillity. Who knows when a comparable faith will be needed again?

PSALM 16

Finally, in *Ps. 16*, another traditional Easter psalm, we have the personal confession by a worshiper of what "covenant" means to him. Here, indeed, all is tranquillity—such tranquillity as could almost appear to a careless reader to be complacency. Too many readers of The Psalms hastily assume that the psalmist writes in such a mood as would have moved the reader to write them. We think that what sounds bloodthirsty to a twentieth-century reader must be meant to be bloodthirsty; that what sounds self-satisfied must come from a complacent heart. This error comes of failing to

remember the distances of time, tongue, and tempera-
ment that separate us from the writers of such lyrics as
this. It is better to believe the best; that way the
meaning becomes clear.

Here, anyhow, is pure contentment. Beginning with a
prayer, "Preserve me, O God," the psalmist goes on to
tell of the joy he has found in being preserved so far. He
may not have deserved such good fortune, but good
fortune it has been indeed. "The lines have fallen for me
in pleasant places," he says (*v.6*)—and in the language
he uses that is as good as saying, "God has given me a
fine house to live in." Just before this he has said, "The
Lord is my chosen portion, and my cup." This is not the
"cup" we mentioned in Ps. 116 above, but the loving cup,
the pledge of friendship and grace that distinguished so
many acts of social worship in the psalmist's religious
tradition. The Lord has shared himself with mankind—
this is his "covenant."

The psalmist then admits, without either shame or
anything recognizable as modesty (modesty being not
regarded by any early Israelite as a virtue anyhow),
that he has, for his part, done his best. God will stay
close to him. It may even be (this is indeed a venture of
faith for an Israelite who has no doctrine of the
afterlife) that God will take care of him after death. At
any rate, he will make sense of death for his faithful
servant. (*V. 10.*) To that brave hope Easter, of course,
gives the real answer. For the psalmist, so far as this life
goes, it is "pleasures for evermore" in the company of
God. With the Christian gospel, that word "evermore" is
given definite content.

Perhaps without that ongoing prayer in the psalm's very first word, "Preserve me," it would have been complacent. But the prayer is still needed; no human virtue is safe. And in any case, is not such pure joy in the company of God infectious?

4. PRAISE

Psalms 33, 66, 146, 30, 32, 103

On the second Sunday following Easter the liturgies of the church direct our thoughts at once to praise. Whether or not we adopt any fixed liturgical order, we are thus reminded that the season of Easter does not end on Easter Day. The joy that Easter brings us continues to resound in the weeks that follow.

The opening psalm of the liturgies for this Sunday is *Ps. 33*. It declares that "the earth is full of the steadfast love of the LORD" (*v. 5*). This psalm could be called the "Now thank we all our God" of the Psalter. It is a psalm for a new year's day—the new year's day of the resurrection.

PSALM 33

The first three verses of this psalm indicate the use that was made of it in Israel's faith. A worshiping congregation is implied in *v. 3*. The musicians are invited to bring out everything they have—we would say to pull out all the organ stops (*v. 2*)—to "play skilfully on the strings, with loud shouts" (*v. 3*). All present are com-

manded to lose themselves in the glory of God and to
communicate the joy of worship.

The next two verses celebrate God's greatness, the
ground of this praise, and the next four (*vs. 6–9*) speak
of God's work in creating all things.

"I believe in God the Father Almighty, Maker of
heaven and earth. . . ." As the ages pass, this article of
faith becomes more, not less, demanding. We, as they,
are called to believe that the universe whose wonders
we are now able to explore with such freedom was
created by a loving and merciful God. We—as they
could not—have seen the face of this Creator in Jesus
Christ. "He spoke, and it came to be." That is the
primary belief, the ground of all praise.

For the Israelite, this creative love was most famil-
iarly known in the preservation of his nation. Therefore,
the psalmist goes on at once to say that God "brings the
counsel of the nations to nought" (*vs. 10–12*), meaning,
as before, the unfriendly and heathen nations. Small,
inconsiderable though the Jewish people might be in
comparison with Assyria, Persia, and Egypt, God is
keeping the faith alive through it. The succeeding
verses (*vs. 13–17*) develop this thought of national
preservation by raising it to a higher level. "The LORD
looks down from heaven" (*v. 13*)—that familiar thought
again, as in Ps. 113—and because of God's concern and
care, "A king is not saved by his great army" (*v. 16*).
And as it has been before, so in the future it will
continue (*vs. 18–19*) if the people will "wait for the
LORD" (*vs. 20–22*).

> O may this bounteous God
> Through all our life be near us,

> With ever joyful hearts
>   And blessed peace to cheer us;
> And keep us in his grace,
>   And guide us when perplexed,
> And free us from all ills
>   In this world and the next.
>
> *—Martin Rinkart, ca. 1636.*
> *Tr. by Catherine Winkworth*

Thus the farthest stretches of belief are brought close to the facts of life as a nation must experience them, and the saving word of God becomes not only a creative command but an invitation to faith.

PSALM 66

Very much the same thoughts are expressed in *Ps. 66*, but in a different dramatic setting. Here we have a psalm in two distinct parts; one is expressed in communal terms (*vs. 1–12*); the other, in personal terms (*vs. 13–20*).

It opens with a phrase that it shares with an even more famous psalm, the Hundredth, a phrase magnificently expressing the enthusiasm of Old Testament faith—"Make a joyful noise to God, all the earth." Let everybody join in, not only the favored people of Israel! What Israel has seen will soon be seen by the whole world. So the singing congregation invites all the peoples to come and see what God has done for Israel. It is first the exodus (*vs. 6–7*) that is brought in evidence, the mightiest of God's historic acts. Then in *vs. 8–12* another deliverance after national catastrophe is extolled, but in this case we do not know which one is referred to. *Verse 12* was much in the minds of British people during the days of World War II, when a new vividness and point was lent to the words, "Thou didst let men ride over our heads; we went through fire and through water."

The second half of the psalm sounds like a solo taking up where the chorus left off, or perhaps a voice representing the worshiping congregation answers the priestly voices from the choir. There is first a vow of worship and allegiance to God (*vs. 13–15*), and then a testimony, inviting all God-fearing people to "come and hear . . . what he has done for me" (*vs. 16–19*). The triumph of the faithful and obedient child of God is that he can introduce others to God as he would to a friend. In the old liturgies verses of this psalm weave themselves in and out of the Easter services, and nothing could be more appropriate at Easter time than the use of this psalm, which lays a nation's faith alongside a personal faith.

PSALM 146

The short and ecstatic *Ps. 146* comes naturally next for our consideration, because it is very much like the second half of Ps. 66. Once again, a man who has found what a change faith makes in his life calls on all who will listen to hear his testimony. Isaac Watts has made of this a memorable and well-known hymn:

> I'll praise my Maker while I've breath;
> And when my voice is lost in death,
>   Praise shall employ my nobler powers.

So just as Ps. 33 says "Blessed is the nation whose God is the LORD," here the singer says "Happy is he whose help is the God of Jacob" (*v. 5*). That other psalm warned the king against putting his trust in a war-horse. This one warns the subjects against godlessly putting their trust in a king—the profound spiritual issue of politics and loyalties that was raised by Samuel (I Sam., ch. 8) when the Israelites first sought to change their constitution and become a settled monarchic society. We shall see later (in Chapter 6) what responsibilities the king bore. In Israel, when its religion was at its best, the responsibilities of kingship exactly balanced the privileges, and the obedience required of a king toward God was the obedience required of his subjects toward him: let the one fail, and the other became meaningless.

The Lord cares for his people (*vs. 7–9*). That is the important thing. Whatever misfortune might overtake a man in this world, however desperate he might be, there is more help in God than he can know. Men's justice may be scanty, but God, in his supreme justice, brings "the way of the wicked . . . to ruin" (*v. 9*).

PSALM 30

Now we come to a rather different climate of faith. *Psalm 30* is headed "A Psalm and Song at the dedication of the house of David" (KJV). This festival was a very late addition to Israel's religious year, being an act of thanksgiving for the deliverance from Syrian bondage under Judas Maccabaeus (165 B.C.). The festival is referred to in John 10:22 as the occasion on which our

Lord spoke his memorable words on the Good Shepherd.

But in its origin, the psalm is a very personal utterance, far in intention from any such public festivity. As such it is most precious, being full of praise, but it is also full of confession. The keynote is sounded at the beginning, where we have words of thanksgiving to God for giving help to a man who had despaired of it (*vs. 1–3*). At once the singer invites his friends to join in his song of praise, and to be assured, from his experience, that "weeping may tarry for the night, but joy comes with the morning" (*vs. 4–5*).

Then comes the confession, expressed in one of those noble paradoxes so characteristic of Old Testament moral meditation. "I was self-confident," he says in effect, "and that was the cause of my despair" (*v. 6*). God had blessed him, and he had accepted this as his right (*v. 7*); so as soon as misfortune came, he was helpless. His grievance toward God expressed itself in a familiar and unlovely way. "If I die," he was saying, "what good will that do me or You?" (*vs. 9–10*).

But once delivered from the misfortune (perhaps the sickness) that evoked these thoughts, the psalmist returns to praise and to renewed vows of faith. He has had, as it were, a glimpse of Easter, of the vistas of God's mercy and judgment, and the glory he has seen has warned him against that self-sufficiency which is death to faith. (*Vs. 11–12.*)

PSALM 32

The brilliant colors of praise show up all the better for a dark background of penitence. Praise is not always

a matter for shouting; it is not the cheers of a
brainwashed, hero-addicted crowd. It is the expression
of the joy of a person who knows what redemption is. In
this world it can be nothing else. This is the theme of *Ps.
32*, called "A Maskil," or "a teaching psalm."

It opens up new dimensions by the use of a single
word in its opening verse: "Blessed is he . . . whose sin
is *covered.*" Now the Hebrew word for "to make
atonement" is *kaphar*, and that means what it sounds
like in English: "cover." In the ancient story of Cain and
Abel in Gen., ch. 4, the Lord says to Cain after the
crime: "What have you done? The voice of your brother's blood is crying to me from the ground." In primitive
days, when blood was spilled, it was thought to be
crying to heaven for vengeance until it was covered up.

But how can a crime or a sin be covered? The
primitive way was to throw earth over the blood. God's
way is to throw love over the sin. The whole story of our
salvation is the story of how covering blood with earth
was transformed into the delicate and searching opera-
tion of atonement—mankind individually and collec-
tively restored to God's confidence; mankind, frightened
of the God it had offended, brought to see that God is
love. The greatest New Testament passage on this is
Heb. 12:18–24, which has been paraphrased in a popular
and vivid evangelical hymn:

> Abel's blood for vengeance
>   Pleaded to the skies,
> But the blood of Jesus
>   For our pardon cries.
> —*From an eighteenth-century Italian hymn.*
>   *Tr. by Edward Caswall*

Psalm 32 is the expression of an individual man's aspiration to these august ideas. He has known suffering, but the secret was this: "When I declared not my sin, my body wasted away" (*v. 3*). When he confessed, then at once there was relief (*v. 5*). If only men will learn to remain close to God while they can, they will not feel that God has left them friendless in the day of misfortune (*v. 6*). He turns to his audience and says in effect (*vs. 8–11*), "As long as you are obstinately self-reliant, you will be helpless as soon as you are unhappy." ("Else it will not keep with you," *v. 9*, is an attempt to translate an obscure phrase which probably intends to convey the idea that, if you are obstinate, God's mercy will seem to have disappeared.)

This beautiful contrast between praise and penitence (complementary conditions, which we find in Ps. 30 and *Ps. 32*) is also to be found in Ps. 31, whose key sentences are "Thou art my God" and "My times are in thy hand" (Ps. 31:14–15). It is this secret of humility that offers the key to peace and praise and that makes a man able to say for himself and to others:

> Be strong, and let your heart take courage,
>   all you who wait for the LORD!
>
>   (Ps. 31:24)

PSALM 103

And so we come to the incomparable *Ps. 103*—so beautiful, so familiar, that comment seems almost superfluous. The glory of this psalm has inspired many hymn writers to paraphrase and imitate it: "Praise, My Soul, the King of Heaven," "Praise Ye the Lord, the

Almighty," and "O Bless the Lord, My Soul" are well-known hymns founded on it.

Psalm 103 is expressed in the first person singular, like the last four we have reviewed. It is based on the personal experience of a singer who now wants to share it with his friends, and who has in fact shared it with untold numbers of people through the ages. It is an "acrostic" (see Chapter 3), offering variations on the theme of thanksgiving.

Verses 1–5 invite us to praise God, facing us at once with God's power to forgive and to heal; *vs. 6–7* acknowledge that this is the experience of all faithful people. Israel's very reason for being a nation is that it is called to proclaim this quality in the living God.

From that point onward the psalm becomes a hymn of all men's experience. The *undeserved* grace of God (*v. 10*) is the miracle. Men have sinned, the nation has sinned, but God has not treated them as they deserved to be treated, or as they, in similar circumstances, would have treated one another. God has shown himself to be a father (*v. 13*) who knows his children and who understands them.

Men feel, understandably, that at times they are "dust" (*v. 14*). "Dust" here means much more than "dust"—powdered particles of rock—in our own speech. It is the "dust" of the "dustbin"—garbage, rubbish. God knows all about that. If we are hopelessly depressed, have lost all interest in life and all sense of purpose—if this has happened to a man, or a nation, God knows it. His knowledge of our being "dust" is not contempt, but compassion. If we are as transitory as the grass and the flowers (*v. 15*), not only has God provided for this; he has given us a "glory" that creatures of eternity could not have. (I Cor. 15:38–41.)

God loves men for being men: this is the unique thought in this psalm. Isaac Watts once wrote a Communion hymn that contains a most memorable stanza:

> The angelic host above
>   Can never taste this food;
> They feast upon a Savior's love,
>   But not a Savior's blood.

That expresses it exactly; it is not true that God would like us better if we were angels or gods. As men we know his love—his mercy, his sacrificial love toward sinners—in a way that no other part of creation can experience it.

No doubt this is why a man can call upon heavenly beings, as though they were his equals, to join in the praise of God:

> Bless the LORD, O you his angels,
>   you mighty ones who do his word.
>   (*V. 20*)

5. PILGRIMAGE

Psalms 84, 42, 43, 120 to 134, 132

Some of the most beautiful and popular of the psalms are associated with the idea and the historical custom of pilgrimage. The background of this takes us to the heart of Israel's history, and we shall pause here to survey it.

In the days of King Josiah (who reigned from 640 to 609 B.C.), which were also the days of the prophet Jeremiah, a religious reform was enacted in Judah. It will be recalled that Judah was the southern half of what had been the United Kingdom of Saul, David, and Solomon, and which thereafter was divided into Judah (with its capital at Jerusalem) and Israel (with its capital at Samaria). After the sack of Samaria in 722 B.C., Judah alone was left as a sovereign state (it later lost its sovereignty to Babylon in the disastrous defeat and deportation of 586 B.C.).

This reform in Judah profoundly affected the life of every faithful citizen from that time to the time of our Lord and, indeed, to the final sack of Jerusalem by the Romans in A.D. 70. The reform was the result of a dramatic discovery. In some forgotten vault in the Temple at Jerusalem, a document was discovered that is believed to be substantially what we have in the book of Deuteronomy. Josiah, zealous for the faith, caused this document to be carefully studied and thereafter read to the people. As a result, many reforms were carried out. The one that concerns us here decreed that the central acts of worship must from that time onward be carried out only at Jerusalem. Worship at the local sanctuaries was, as it were, downgraded, and many of them were closed altogether.

Now in our Lord's time Jewish worship had taken on a dual rhythm. On the one hand there was the teaching worship of the local synagogue; on the other, the august sacrificial worship of the Temple. But synagogue worship did not develop until long after Josiah's time, and much heartburning and controversy were caused by the rigor of this requirement that every faithful Jew must go to Jerusalem for the major festivals of the Jewish year. This was a cause of suffering to Jeremiah in his early years. His father was a local and dispossessed priest, but the young Jeremiah was in favor of the reforms. (The reader may wish to look back at the comments on Ps. 69, in Chapter 1, with this in mind.)

But as things developed down to our Lord's time, the gatherings at Jerusalem became delightful, dramatic, and festive occasions to which people came from all the places into which Jews had been dispersed through the ages of their country's stormy history. Jerusalem was crowded to the rooftops on these high days, and everybody was full of joy and hope. Not the least among the factors contributing to the excitement was the physical situation of Jerusalem, which, being some 2,500 feet above sea level, involved, by the route most usually followed via Jericho, some 3,200 feet of climbing in less than a dozen miles. High up in the hills, the Holy City remained invisible until one had passed over the lip of the "saucer" in which it actually stood. From the city, the surrounding hills looked like bastions. From the plain, the city itself was still an invisible promise. The whole journey was one of faith and hope: sight came only at the last minute.

This is the background of that string of little jewels which we call the pilgrim psalms, Ps. 120 to 134. Before turning to them, however, we shall consider two other very well known psalms which are best understood in this context.

PSALM 84

"How lovely is thy dwelling place"—with this haunting phrase, which has kindled the imagination of a score of poets and musicians, begins this most beautiful of all the celebrations of pilgrimage in the Psalter. The poet is, as it were, on his way to Jerusalem for one of the feasts. He speaks of his love for the place, his longing for it. Anywhere else he feels like an exile. Living in the heathen country where he dwells, he would give his life itself (*v. 10*) for a day in the Temple; he would forfeit all his prosperity for a church cleaner's job that would enable him to live in the Temple. He can envy the birds that nest among its pinnacles (*v. 3*), and especially the choristers whose work takes them daily into the sanctuary (*v. 4*). He looks at the dusty road, at a milestone reading, as it were, "Jerusalem 45 miles." He feels thirsty, and longs to come upon one of the rare oases in the desert (*vs. 5–7*). Then he thinks: "But I am lucky! The 'highways to Zion' are in my heart." He says to himself the prayers he learned in his youth, including a prayer for the king (*vs. 8–9*). And all along the road he sings, "Blessed is the man who trusts in thee!"

To understand the psalm, all that is needed is to see the worship of the Temple as carrying with it, for the ordinary worshiper, all the excitement of a holiday. There is no other word for it. This is a holy season, a season of reunion and of social pleasure, a long journey with a promise at its end.

PSALMS 42; 43

To see it from the other end, so to speak, look in *Ps. 42* and *43*, which are one single psalm artificially divided by ancient editors. Here is a man who for some reason—it rather looks as if he is some kind of political prisoner or exile—has to watch others setting out for the holiday on which he may not go himself. His distress is exactly proportionate to the joy expressed in Ps. 84.

"My soul thirsts for God," he says (*42:2*). "My soul longs, yea, faints," says Ps. 84; but that other psalmist knows that his thirst is to be satisfied. This one does not know how long he must go on being thirsty. People mock him (*42:3*), and memories pierce him (*42:4*). The majestic scenery of the Jordan Valley at its northern end (*42:6*) gives him no comfort; the roaring of the river over the rocks (*42:7*) arouses only melancholy echoes in his mind.

He says his prayers (*42:8*) and sings his psalms; but he breaks off and says, "Why hast thou forgotten me?"

(*42:9;* cf. Ps. 22:1). Unbelievers continue to taunt him. (*42:10.*) At last he confronts God squarely. (*43:1–2.*) "Is this fair?" he says. (Look back at what is said about Ps. 54 in Chapter 1.) Will not God arise and vindicate him and set him free? It all pours out in a passionate prayer—"Oh send out thy light and thy truth; let them lead me." If only this can happen, nobody at the festival will sing more fervent praise than he.

The refrain (*42:5, 11;43:5*) interrupts the lament with poignant effect. The first time it is followed by a lapse into grief; the second time it is followed by a resolution, Job-like, to stand on his own feet and defend himself before God. The third time it emerges from an act of submission and praise. Such is the rhythm and pattern of human life. "Hope in God"—this is not always an aspiration that we can fulfill, however fervently we say the words. But even solitary prayer and praise can generate faith, so that what begins as a helpless cry can become a firm and confident creed. Though he may not follow the highway to Zion with his feet, there it is, all the time, in his heart.

PSALMS 120 TO 134

Only a word is needed about each of the pilgrim psalms. We may suppose that all of them, except perhaps Ps. 132, were folk songs that came from various sources and periods but that became associated, simply because of their brevity and conciseness, with the pilgrimages to Jerusalem. That they were popular favorites (as a few of them still are) need not be doubted. It is especially fruitful to imagine what they

meant to our Lord and his friends when they made their
regular journeys to Jerusalem with all the other faithful
of Israel.

For example, there is Ps. 121, whose opening words
are a picture of the pilgrims climbing the steep path,
and whose second verse is the first article in the Jewish,
as, indeed, in the Christian creed: "My help comes from
the LORD, who made heaven and earth." Help comes not
from the hills but from him who made them. At once the
joy of Ps. 122 follows—the holiday song, wherein we
hear of the worshiper's pleasure in being with his
"brethren and companions," his love for the honored
city, and his prayer for its peace. Once he is over the top
of the hill, and going down the gentle slope toward the
gate, he will perhaps sing Ps. 125, with its memorable
geographical simile: "As the mountains are round about
Jerusalem, so the LORD is round about his people." And
as the crowd thickens, and more and more old friends'
faces are seen, he will move on to Ps. 133, in which he
sings of the pleasures of unity and friendship.

In Ps. 127 and 128 he sings of the personal blessings
the Lord has given him; these psalms are songs of the
family. In Ps. 123 and 131 he will sing of his ideals for
himself—a song of humility—"Like a child quieted at its
mother's breast; like a child that is quieted is my soul."

Inevitably, with his companions, he will sing some of
the patriotic songs that recall the varied, tragic, but
spiritually triumphant, history of his people—the magnificently virile Ps. 124, the violent and bitter Ps. 129,
and the tender, wistful Ps. 126.

Perhaps Ps. 126 is the most beautiful piece of
literature in the whole series. It opens with a reference

to some deliverance from disaster: "When God delivered us, it was like a dream—unbelievable!" And it closes with a prayer that deliverance may come again to a people who are like a dried-up watercourse, longing for the refreshment of freedom and release from anxiety. The pilgrim could sing songs like these whether or not the time of his singing them was a time of national crisis; they reminded him of God's goodness and nourished his faith in God's future providence.

In the same way, he could sing a highly personal utterance like Ps. 120, which sounds like the exasperated prayer of some exhausted statesman, or some magistrate or governor who is moved to say, "I am for peace; but when I speak, they are for war!" (Ps. 120:7)—and that indeed has a contemporary sound today.

And surely Ps. 130 must have been precious to him, the profoundest religious utterance of the collection. It is a fundamentally joyful psalm, beginning in the dark, demon-infested depths of life and ending with a shout of hope, confessing man's undeserving condition and proclaiming faith in God's readiness to forgive him. And so, after singing of all these truths and experiences, he holds out his hand to his neighbor and says, in Ps. 134, "Come with me to praise the Lord."

Laying Ps. 132 aside for the moment, we have in these psalms tiny epigrams of religious experience that have been the inspiration of the saints for two thousand years and more. Psalm 130, for example, kept Martin Luther sane when he was standing trial at Wittenberg; and it was hearing an anthem setting of it in St. Paul's, London, that set up in John Wesley's mind the thoughts

that, on the same evening, May 24, 1738, exploded into
conviction and conversion. The history of the Scottish
Covenanters is full of references to Ps. 124.

More recently, Ps. 124 and 133 played a central part
in a dramatic Scottish gesture of church reconciliation.
In 1843 the Church of Scotland had split almost down
the middle on doctrinal points, and the two churches
continued in uneasy separation from that date for
eighty-six years. Then on a certain day in 1929, the two
churches came together again, and two immense symbolic processions converged on St. Giles' Cathedral,
Edinburgh, moving through the ancient streets of the
town, singing the metrical versions of Ps. 124 and 133 as
they marched.

But if one thinks of our Lord and his friends joining
in the procession to Jerusalem—what then? "My help
comes from the LORD" (Ps. 121:2); six days later they
are going to hear the scoffers saying, "He trusts in God;
let God deliver him now" (Matt. 27:43). They must have
sung, "Pray for the peace of Jerusalem!" (Ps. 122:6);
and Luke records that "when he drew near and saw the
city he wept over it, saying, 'Would that even today you
knew the things that make for peace!' " (Luke 19:41–
42). Jesus, alone of all that throng of holidaymakers
that day, knew that if the joys, the hopes, the confidence, the aspirations in the pilgrim psalms were to
come true for the world, he himself must forgo the joys,
reenact the sufferings, manifest the faith in desolation,
and in his own person make the whole journey from the
utmost depths to the height of God's presence. The
pilgrim psalms celebrate all human life, but they are a
drama of the cross as well. In particular, Ps. 130 is a

complete story, not only of the salvation we look for, but also of the salvation Christ procured.

PSALM 132

The pilgrim psalms are both personal and public. Every so often they break out in a refrain such as "Our help is in the name of the LORD . . ." or, "Let Israel now say . . ." or, "O Israel, hope in the LORD!" *Psalm 132* is different from the others in being relatively lengthy, dramatic, and liturgical. It is nonetheless in a popular style. Its second half (*vs. 11–18*) answers its first half (*vs. 1–10*) by showing how, in the promises of God, recorded history will repeat itself. The story about David is the story of the finding of the Ark after it had been confiscated by the Philistines. The Ark was a modest chest in which lay the most sacred object known to Israel, the table of the Law. In the Law, God had revealed himself to his people, and they almost felt that God was personally present in the Ark. The loss of it was the loss of their dearest prize, and the loss of their very reason for living. The story of the loss of the Ark and of its return is marvelously told in I Sam. 4:10 to 7:2. It was when the Ark was taken away that the mother of Phinehas' son named the child Ichabod, saying "The glory has departed from Israel!" (I Sam. 4:21); and it was when it was brought up again to the sanctuary that David danced before the Lord (II Sam. 6:16–23). *Psalm 132* goes over that great story again, telling how David swore that he would have the Ark back in its proper place, and how "we heard of it in Ephrathah, we found it in the fields of Jaar" (*v. 6*). Jaar is "Kiriath-jearim" in I Sam. 7:2, a frontier village; and Ephrathah is a village that was also called Bethlehem. (This is why this psalm has anciently been associated with Christmas Day.)

The second half of the psalm allegorizes the historic facts of the first half; taking up again the thought of *vs. 9–10*, it says that what God did then, he will always do for "David"—meaning the people of David's country. And it will be a son of David who leads his people to their true fulfillment (cf. Ps. 89:3–4; another Christmas psalm).

Despite its differences from the other pilgrim psalms, *Ps. 132* is not in the least out of place among them, for the Temple to which the pilgrims are going is the throne of David (Ps. 122:5). In Holy Week, the people shout to Jesus, "Blessed is the kingdom of our father David that is coming!" (Mark 11:10). The one thing that we do not have in the pilgrim psalms is a reference to Moses and the exodus. But this is because, whereas Moses is the timeless symbol of faith and moral rectitude (and the exodus the revelation of this to the people), David is the other pillar of belief—the symbol of victory. And it was on these great holidays that the common people shared in the promise of God's victory.

6. ROYALTY

Psalms 98, 93, 96, 97, 99, 100, 72, 144, 101

The psalms to be considered in this chapter are psalms of enthronement, in which the image of "the king" is especially prominent. Nowadays it requires a good deal of imagination to re-create the image of royalty as Israel understood it, but the first thing to notice is a helpful point from Israel's history. Only a small minority of sovereign states in the Northern Hemisphere retain a monarchy today, and even in these the mystique of monarchy has largely faded. But it should be remembered that if we take the history of ancient Israel as extending from the exodus to A.D. 70, we have a period of about 1,300 years, during only about a third of which Israel had a king, in the sense of a sovereign, at all.

Kings such as the notorious Herods were, of course, vassals of Rome. The last genuine king of Judah was Josiah, who died in battle in 609 B.C. Two so-called kings, puppets of Babylon, followed him, but the whole political structure in Judah collapsed in 586 B.C. So in a sense, when the image of the king was applied to God, the Jews of our Lord's time were also forced to use their imagination.

It was David and Solomon who inaugurated (in the tenth century B.C.) the high tradition of the king who was also priest. Israel was always deeply conscious of the hazards of absolute monarchy. Its aspirations in respect to the righteous king, the protector of his people, are best expressed in beautiful words attributed to David himself at the end of his life (II Sam. 23:3–4):

> When one rules justly over men,
>   ruling in the fear of God,
> he dawns on them like the morning light,
>   like the sun shining forth upon a cloudless
>   morning,
>   like rain that makes grass to sprout
>   from the earth.

Therefore, however grossly a human king might fail of such ideals as these, it was customary at his coronation to express the highest hopes for him and to ascribe the highest virtues to him. The language used in coronation hymns of this kind was so exalted that with very little adaptation it could be applied to God himself. Perfect righteousness, such as was formally ascribed to the new king, was, Israel knew perfectly well, to be found only in God. It was he who was really the people's defender and the upholder of justice. It was his rule which provided that stability and peace in which righteousness could flourish. In human terms the need for stability is expressed in a famous verse at the very end of The Book of Judges (Judg. 21:25): "In those days there was no king in Israel; every man did what was right in his own eyes." But Israel really knew that the one King who could certainly establish peace and order was none other than God himself.

We turn now to a series of psalms that are adaptations of coronation songs for use in public worship.

PSALM 98

This simple song of victory is particularly appropriate to Easter—and recognized as such by some liturgies of the church. The king is returning home from a victory—perhaps not to be enthroned for the first time, but returning to a throne too long left empty. He has vindicated himself (v. 2), shown his enemies what he is made of. He has shown his people that they were right to trust him. That situation is at once translated into the religious mode by ascribing a similar victory to God. The people (v. 4), led by the musicians (vs. 5–6), are called to join in God's praise, and all nature (vs. 7–9) is invited to join in also.

That is the simplest form of the pattern; other psalms produce variations on it.

PSALM 93

"The LORD reigns"! This short and vivid psalm is concerned with one point—the superiority of God's power (expressed as kingly power) over every other power, natural or supernatural. Just as the king might be viewed as the principle of the *people's* safety, so God is the principle of the *universe's* safety. The idea of the world "established [so that] it shall never be moved" (v.

1) is not a barbarous pre-astronomical error. It is a
celebration of God's power as the principle of order
throughout the universe, however immense the universe
turns out to be.

The Lord's enemies are here represented by "the
floods" (*v. 3*). In Jewish imagination, large masses of
water, troubled by storm, are a favorite symbol of
suffering and anxiety. The Lord in his wisdom is
mightier than these. The ground of all worship is the
peace which, in the presence of this serene wisdom, is
made known to the believer (*v. 5*).

PSALM 96

The leading thought here is that God, or the King, is
the Judge of all the earth. In the foreground is the
controversy between God and "the gods" (*vs. 4–5;* cf. Ps.
95:3): "the gods" are anything that the heathen may
believe in. The living God, who made all things (*v. 5*), is
he who alone can be worshiped (cf. Ps. 115 and the First
Commandment, Ex. 20:1–3). Therefore, it is right that
God, like a victorious king, should demand tribute from
all peoples (*vs. 7–8*), and that those who worship him
should present themselves "in holy array" (*v. 9*). The
attractive expression in the older versions, "the beauty
of holiness," is not an abstraction, as it is sometimes
thought to be. It refers to the vestments, expressing the
joy of worship, worn by the priests, and metaphorically
worn by all who are with them.

The last verses of the psalm (*vs. 10–13*) express again
the security that the faithful feel in God's presence. Just
as "the world is established" (*v. 10;* cf. Ps. 93 above), so

justice will be established. All the evils with which this
world is burdened—oppression, waste, and folly—will
disappear when the Lord's Kingdom is proclaimed.

Two Christian associations of this psalm show how it
has built itself into the church's worship. The first is the
association of *vs. 7–9* with Epiphany—that is, with the
tribute of love brought to the infant King by the Men of
the East (Matt. 2:10–11). The other is the result of a
strange piece of sanctified forgery. Copying out this
psalm in Latin, some nameless Christian scribe was
writing the words of *v. 10: Dicite inter gentes, Dominus
regnat.* ("Say among the nations, 'The LORD reigns!' ")
The temptation to add the words *a ligno* ("from the
tree") was so great that he slipped them into his copy,
and they became part of the psalm in one of the church's
traditions: "Say among the nations, 'The Lord reigns
from the tree.' " The psalmist, of course, would not have
said that; but it is what Christians know when they sing
the psalm. And the expression found its way into the
most majestic of all Passiontide hymns, "The Royal
Banners Forward Go," whose original Latin writer in
the sixth century ended his poem with the Latin
translated by these lines:

> Fulfilled is now what David told
> In true prophetic song of old;
> To all the nations, "Lo," saith he,
> "Our God is reigning from the tree."
> —*Venantius Fortunatus, ca. 530–609.*
> *Tr. by John Mason Neale et al.*

PSALM 97

Here the enthronement of God is to be associated
with the great mystery of Sinai. Shame to the idolators

(*v. 7*), joy for the faithful (*v. 8*), are the consequences of God's tremendous appearing—of a theophany. Out of this comes the true moral experience of man. (*Vs. 10–12.*) This is the experience recorded in Exodus: the Ten Commandments, God's moral self-revelation, come out of the fire and passion of religious encounter, not out of somebody's tranquil philosophizings.

The King, as author of moral rectitude, is a figure of massive mystery. God the King is surrounded by "clouds and thick darkness." This is one of the Psalter's profoundest moments. It may well move a Christian to two thoughts. One is that no morality proceeding from any authority less than that of Sinai is worth following. The psalms may sound very cultic and primitive, but the moral sense in them comes from an experience whose only adequate picture is of a flaming mountain.

Secondly, Heb. 12:18–24 reminds us that the revelation that in the days of the exodus was too holy for mortal sight has now been given to us in Christ; that the beauty of God, veiled then by merciful clouds from eyes which it would have blinded, is now veiled in the flesh of Jesus. Therefore, Christians miss the whole truth—they fail to understand both the Old Testament and the New—if they do not see in Jesus the vision from which their morality may be derived.

PSALM 99

The same atmosphere of grandeur and infinite beauty surrounds *Ps. 99*. Once again, the judgment and enthronement of God must induce fear in all who do not believe, but joy in those who wait for him. As God spoke unmistakably in the events of the exodus (*vs. 6–7*), so he speaks in his justice and righteousness through all the ages (*vs. 4–5*). "Thou wast a forgiving God to them, but an avenger of their wrongdoings" (*v. 8*). This is justice surrounded by glory. It is summed up in the chorus: "Extol the LORD our God; worship at his footstool! Holy is he!" (*vs. 5, 9*).

PSALM 100

And then comes the Hundredth Psalm, the origin of one of the most famous of hymns in English, "All People That on Earth Do Dwell," and second only to the Twenty-third Psalm in popularity. All it does is to call on all creation to worship the Lord, its King and its Maker. Here is pure worship, and joy in worship. The Lord, like the king, is shepherd of his people (*v. 3*), and, as the psalmists so often repeat, "His steadfast love endures for ever" (*v. 5*).

These cheerful songs are probably very ancient in their origin. If we may trust a Biblical editor, it seems that Ps. 96, with part of Ps. 105, was sung when David brought up the Ark to Jerusalem (cf. Ps. 132, in Chapter 5, and see also I Chron. 16:23–34).

But finally we may turn to a psalm of somewhat different form, Ps. 72, in which the imagery of the coronation is much more prominent.

PSALM 72

This psalm, whose second part (*vs. 8–20*) is the origin of the famous hymns "Jesus Shall Reign Where'er the

Sun" and "Hail to the Lord's Anointed," is originally a prayer of intercession for a king at his enthronement. In it we see amply expressed those ideals of kingship which we mentioned earlier. Two points are especially insisted on: the hope that justice will reign with the new king and that all oppression will be ended (*vs. 2–4, 12–14*), and the hope that the reign will be long and that prosperity will attend it (*vs. 5–11, 15-17*). Vivid imagery contributes to the vitality of the picture. The description of the expected joys is almost exactly in the language of II Sam. 23:3–4. The extent of the king's dominion is expressed as the total extent of the known earth. Fantastic and beautiful exaggerations abound. The richest countries beyond Israel's borders will bring their wealth into the country. (*Vs. 10–11;* cf. Isa., ch. 60.) The good harvests will stand as tall as the tallest trees in the known world, the cedars of Lebanon (*v. 16*).

When Israel adapted this psalm for use as a hymn, the editorial work was done somewhat less thoroughly than it would have been in later times. Here we are still praying for the king; and of course we cannot pray for the living God. (Isaac Watts perpetuated this anomaly by writing, in "Jesus Shall Reign Where'er the Sun": "For him shall endless prayer be made"—a strange notion that some hymnal editors seek to correct by substituting "To him" for "For him.") But the real point is this: when these aspirations were expressed on behalf of a human king, they were dreams, but when they are expressed in the worship of God, they are promises.

PSALM 144

It is worth taking a brief glance at a coronation song, *Ps. 144*, designed originally to be sung by a victorious king himself. Inevitably it was ascribed to David. The king speaks as a man of war (*vs. 1–11*), in language somewhat overviolent for contemporary taste, yet realistic in his time. But at the end the promises for the new reign of peace are most beautifully expressed: "May our sons in their youth be like plants full grown, our daughters like corner pillars cut for the structure of a palace; . . . may there be no cry of distress in our streets!" (*vs. 12, 14*). Here the clue is given openly: "Happy the people whose God is the LORD!" (*v. 15;* cf. Ps. 33:12).

Our generation knows as well as Israel how barren are hopes of peace and godly prosperity for any whose god is not the Lord who manifested himself in Christ.

PSALM 101

Finally, we may refer to another psalm designed to be sung by the king as a prayer of petition for himself. This is the king's personal response to his people's hopes. He promises to live in integrity in his own house (*v. 2*), to keep himself from evil (*vs. 3–4*), to give due reward to righteousness, and to root out corruption from public life (*vs. 5–8*). The occasional violence of its language is no more than an expression of the completeness of the king's dedication to goodness—just as the violence in Ps. 144 expresses his dedication to his people's peace and safety. Having begun with the public praises offered to a king, we fittingly end with a king's self-dedication. Here we have a psalm that cannot be applied to God in the sense that Ps. 96 to 100 can be, but one that expresses the faith before God of a righteous man of authority. These psalms bring us close to our Lord's conception of royalty as obedience to God and service to man.

7. NATURE

Psalms 104, 29, 147, 148, 65, 67

In many parts of the church the fifth Sunday after Easter is kept as a day on which prayers are offered for those who work on the land. This tradition, whether or not we follow it in our own church, suggests that we might look at some psalms associated with Israel's thought about that which we call "nature."

For modern urban man there is an assumed distinction between the countryside and the town. It is widely (and quite wrongly) believed that it is in the country that one sees the handiwork of God, whereas in the town God's handiwork is defaced by man. This is romantic and inaccurate. A bad farmer can bully the soil and deface God's work; and a scientist or a technician or a builder in the town is working all the time within a natural framework established by the Creator.

There have been many views about "nature" through which Western man has passed. There is the view that nature is corrupt and must be sanctified by grace. There is the view that what is natural is noble, and that sophistication is always identical with corruption. There is the view that nature is for relaxation, and cities are for work—and so you go to the country for holidays, and to the towns for your living. No one of these has any basis in the Old Testament. The Old Testament mind found three truths about nature to ponder: (1) Nature is in itself majestic and terrifying, but God, its Creator, can rejoice in it; (2) nature is an area in which God manifests his power as terrible and yet redemptive; and (3) nature is chancy and unpredictable, so that when it works in a manner favorable to man, it may well be a sign that God is pleased with man, and when it works against him, that God is displeased. Although there may be diseases, droughts, famines, and accidents, there is no other source of man's livelihood, and nature provides much to be thankful for.

PSALM 104

For sheer grandeur, this psalm (the origin of the hymn "O Worship the King All-glorious Above") is unrivaled in the Psalter. It is like a colorful paraphrase of Gen., ch. 1; it contains thoughts that are found in Job, chs. 38 to 41. It is outward-looking and massively serene.

There is little in it that is not self-explanatory; oddly enough, one of the few slight difficulties, for those who know the older versions, appears very near the beginning. The first four verses begin where Gen., ch. 1, begins—in the heavens. In *Ps. 104:4* the KJV reads, "Who maketh his angels spirits; his ministers a flaming fire," and that phrase, which is more mysterious than meaningful, was one of the reasons why the psalm became associated with Pentecost. (*Verses 29–30* provide much better ground for that association, and they present no problem as to the actual text.) The true meaning of *v. 4* is found in the RSV, which substitutes "messengers" for "angels," and "winds" for "spirits," and also turns subject and predicate the other way around, so that we read, "who makest the winds thy messengers, fire and flame thy ministers [servants]."

Then, again like Gen., ch. 1, the psalm moves to the earth (*v. 5;* cf. Ps. 93:1), and then at once to the waters (*vs. 6–9*), whose receding left the dry land open to sight. Then follows a fascinating catalog of the living creatures (*vs. 10–22*), ending with the unforgettable picture of man as he "goes forth to his work and to his labor until the evening" (*v. 23*). In *vs. 24–35* the poet acknowledges the dependence of all living things on God for their food, their life, and their happiness, with which, at the last moment, he contrasts the unhappiness of those who do not see all of this as the creation of a wise and loving God.

Primitive literature in other religions provides parallels to this psalm. It seems to echo especially lines reputedly composed by an Egyptian pharaoh. Here the psalmist is sharing a delight in creation that is felt by any sensitive creature; but the difference is that he refers it all *to the one God of Israel.*

PSALM 29

Here is a very different approach to nature. In *Ps. 29* nature is seen as the field in which God speaks with power. When nature is terrifying, it reminds men of the terrible voice of God. After a liturgical opening (in which we hear again the famous text we met in Ps.

96:9), the poet sings of the "voice" of God that to primitive man is first heard in terror. Thunders, floods, earthquakes that shake the mountains and throw about the giant redwoods of the ancient world like match-sticks (*vs. 3–6*), the portents of the wilderness (*vs. 7–8*, where Kadesh means the wilderness of Sinai)—these are the signs of a power that, terrible to unregenerate man, is peace to the faithful, and a summons to worship (*vs. 9–11*).

In *v. 9* we have another ambiguous text; the RSV says, "The voice of the LORD makes the oaks to whirl." The marginal reading, which older versions followed, says, "The voice of the LORD makes the hinds to calve." Either way, it is an imaginative detail expressing the terror that nature feels when God speaks. It is the peace of *v. 11* that is contrasted with this primitive terror. But the leading thought is the voice, or the word, of God. Turn for a moment to the opening of the preceding psalm:

> If thou be silent to me,
>   I [shall] become like those who go down
>   to the Pit.
>
>   (Ps. 28:1)

Thus is a truth illuminated by its opposite. The voice of God may be terrible, but it is creative. It is the source of life. God's word is a redemptive word. If God were to keep silent, then a man's fate would be worse than death itself. The silence of God is a greater terror than that Voice which, to the redeemed, is the voice of majesty and of peace.

PSALM 147

If nature can remind man of God's power, both terrifying and redemptive, it can also remind him of God's providence. In *Ps. 147* we see the idea of the power and glory of nature associated with that of national security and the establishment of peace. "The LORD builds up Jerusalem" (*v. 2*)—that is the leading thought. To a people who had so much experience of being overrun by ruthless enemies, the very existence of Jerusalem as an inhabited city, and as the center of continuing worship, was a standing miracle. By our Lord's time, two mighty temples had gone down to dust (Solomon's, plundered and burned in 586 B.C.; Zerubbabel's, dismantled ca. 20 B.C.), and the third, Herod's, then a marvel of modern architecture, was destined to follow them within a generation. But a temple was there when the people sang this psalm, after their return from exile, and it stood as a memorial of God's preserving providence.

This, the psalmist goes on to say, is the Lord who provides rain for the earth, food for men and beasts, and joy for those who love him (*vs. 7–11*); it is also the God whose power is seen in nature's austere manifestations (*vs. 16–18*). Just as he sends forth ice, storm, and snow, so he sends forth the word of peace (cf. Isa. 55:10–11; Ps. 122:6; 29:11).

PSALM 148

The same thought is really the basis of *Ps. 148*, but here it is kept for the last two verses. What goes before is a very remarkable piece of literature indeed. This psalm, a celebration of God as the Creator of everything from angels (*v. 2*) to caterpillars (*v. 10*), has inspired many Christian hymn writers—Francis of Assisi in his "Hymn to the Sun" ("All Creatures of Our God and King"), the anonymous author of "Praise the Lord, Ye Heavens Adore Him," and many others. But it was long before the Christian era that it began its journey of inspiration.

Those who know the canticle *Benedicite, Omnia Opera* ("O All Ye Works of the Lord, Bless Ye the Lord")—appointed in the Anglican Book of Common Prayer as an alternative to the *Te Deum* at morning prayer—will at once recognize in it a poem based on this psalm. Its language is an amalgam of *Ps. 148* with verses of Ps. 147. That canticle appears in the Greek (but not the Hebrew) version of The Book of Daniel, and therefore it is not in the canonical Old Testament. It is put into the mouth of the three brave men in Nebuchadnezzar's furnace; and very near the end it has a verse, "O Ananias, Azarias, and Misael, bless ye the Lord . . ." —these being the Greek names of the three legendary heroes, Shadrach, Meshach, and Abednego. That edifying tradition shows how thoughts of God the Creator upheld three men who were suffering violence at the hands of nature's most terrifying instrument—fire.

And there is a story told of Francis of Assisi, whose very life was an acting out of *Ps. 148*. When he was in danger of losing his sight, he had to have an eye cauterized with a red-hot stake. As the fire approached his eye, he said simply, "Brother Fire, be kind to me."

Putting together the story of Francis and that of the

three brave men, with whom, in the fire which left them unscathed, a fourth figure was seen "like the Son of God" (Dan. 3:25, KJV), we have some intimation of the secret that Christ has revealed about nature. He who unswervingly loves God, as Jesus did, has nothing to fear, and everything to enjoy, in his humble and expectant encounters with the forces of nature.

PSALM 65

Psalm 65 is a psalm of thanksgiving, originally composed (almost certainly) after the end of a drought. Drought and famine are still grievously familiar to people who live where this psalm was composed and sung. It took a man of God to discern in the rhythms of nature the hand of God. The beautiful description of the return of fertility to a barren land (*vs. 9–13*) is used as an exhortation to worship. A God who can do such things, and show such mercy, is the proper object of the whole world's worship (*v. 2*) and the joy of those who have found him (*v. 4*). Men need not hope that nature will always be kind; it may be rough and demanding (*vs. 5–8*), but if men will read it rightly, they will find a peace that refreshes and heartens.

PSALM 67

The same thought is found in *Ps. 67*, a cheerful, popular, and from the first, no doubt, congregational psalm. It is a prayer to God to supply the needs of ordinary people. Thanks are given (*v. 6*) for the fruits of the earth and for blessings received and remembered.

Men and nations who continually praise God (*vs. 3, 5*) will find the good hand of God leading them through the barren places and rewarding their patience. The Lord judges fairly (*v. 4*) and shepherds his people; no one who thinks God has forgotten to be just or gracious can be right.

In these ways do the psalms disperse superstition and fear about nature. Nature worship can be the cruelest of religions. Indeed, the idolatries against which psalmists and prophets aimed their denunciations were, as often as not, nature worship. But the secret of peace with nature is peace with God.

8. CARE

Psalms 47, 24b, 8, 2, 110, 27, 23

This is the season of the ascension. At this time Christians think of Christ as the Savior who has finished his work, despite all the world's attempts to frustrate it. Thus they think in pictures that suggest a king returning victorious from battle, enthroned on the rejoicing of his people.

It is psalms of enthronement, then, such as those which we considered in Chapter 6, that are most seasonable. To some extent we shall here be continuing the line of thought that Chapter 7 interrupted. But we shall go farther; because of the ascension we can think not only of the glory achieved, but also of the long journey that went before it. We shall conclude the study with the Twenty-third Psalm. This is, for many, the finest summary of the meaning of Christ's work.

PSALM 47

After all that we have said about Ps. 96 to 100, this psalm needs little explanation. Like them, it is a psalm of enthronement, associated with the new year covenant festival, and illustrating the power of God through the image of the newly enthroned king. But unlike Ps. 96 to 100, this psalm is entirely about God; the "king" is no more than an image and has no reference to any human king. But the coronation is there in all its details—the ceremonial trumpets (v. 5), the captive kings of the subject nations (v. 9), the symbolic shields representing the king's protective power (v. 9; cf. II Chron. 12:9–10), and above all, the long procession *up* the Temple steps (v. 5). All of this is easily absorbed into the language of the church, in its rejoicing at the completion of Christ's work.

PSALM 24:7–10

Even more dramatic, however, is *Ps. 24*, in whose second part we see a victorious king returning from battle. (We shall consider its first part in Chapter 13.) "The strife is o'er, the battle done"—that is the keynote. In this fragment of dramatic worship we have the ceremonial responses that proceed between the leaders of singing and the massed crowds waiting for the king's procession to arrive.

So familiar is the exhortation, "Lift up your heads, O ye gates," that few have any difficulty in understanding its strange use of words. The meaning intended is, presumably, a superlative of "Open up!" The greatness of the king is such that the massive city gates are too small to admit him, colossal though they may be. It is typical of the hyperbole of Hebrew poetry to say, in effect, "If gates can move in any direction other than horizontally, let them do so now."

In some church traditions—preeminently in that of Scotland—this fragment of *Ps. 24* accompanies the bringing in of the elements at the service of Communion. In Scotland it is sung in a metrical form in a hymn beginning, "Ye gates, lift up your heads on high." In the background there is a memory of the text in Rev. 3:20, "Behold, I stand at the door and knock." The imagery reflects exactly the paradox of the Sacrament. The King makes himself small enough to enter so tiny a gate; the loftiest city gates imaginable are insufficient to admit such glory. From a distance Israel received an intimation of that revelation which we have seen in the grandeur and the humility of Christ.

PSALM 8

Like the two preceding psalms, *Ps. 8* is sometimes associated with the celebration of the ascension (as in the Anglican Book of Common Prayer). It is a song of praise to God the Creator, following at first the lines of the so-called "nature" psalms (see Chapter 7), but suddenly taking a turn that makes it unique in the Psalter. It is as if, reading Gen., ch. 1, the poet had stopped to ponder especially Gen. 1:26: man made in God's image, with dominion over nature. Man is "little less than God" (*Ps. 8:5*)—or, in the KJV, "a little lower than the angels" (which comes to almost the same thing). In the great prelude to The Letter to the Hebrews, the unique and divine nature of Christ is interpreted through this and other psalms (see Heb., chs. 1; 2:5–8). Only of Christ can it be said, "Let all God's angels worship him" (Heb. 1:6; cf. Ps. 97:7). Jesus in his resurrection has shown his authority over all things; in his life he showed man what man's authority ought to be.

"Thou hast given him dominion . . ." (*v. 6*). That fateful saying can best be interpreted by going to the place in the Gospels where we read that, after the stilling of the storm, the disciples asked: "Who is this, that even the wind and sea obey him?" (The KJV is almost better here: "What manner of man is this . . . ?") Jesus showed that the secret of dominion—loving, harmonious, ordered dominion over nature—is obedience to God the Father. The psalmist has seen something of this, since he is moved by the immensity of the natural universe to ask, "What is man that thou art mindful of him?" Humility of this kind would enable man to be well on the way toward solving the grievous problems that his greed and arrogance have imposed on the world of nature. Man's fear generates ferocity in animals—why must he fear? Man's hasty greed parches the earth and wastes its products—but why must he be so anxious? Jesus said that birds and flowers can teach a good lesson in dispelling anxiety (Matt. 6:24–34). The obedience of Christ is the pattern to be followed by those who administer the vineyard of God.

PSALM 2

In that same passage in Hebrews, the first of the series of texts quoted to demonstrate the divinity of Christ is from *Ps. 2:* "Thou art my Son, today I have begotten thee" (Heb. 1:5; *Ps. 2:7*). This is strictly an Easter psalm, but it is equally appropriate to ascension.

The central point here is that historically the psalm is relevant to the coronation of a new king after the death of a predecessor who has left behind him a sense of disappointment or disillusionment. There has been a conspiracy against the king and his people (*vs. 1–3*)—a sign of a weak reign. This must be brought to an end (*vs. 4–6*) because it is a conspiracy against God himself. The king has the right to rule not only over Israel but over the whole world. He proposes to exercise this right (*vs. 6–9*), and the conspirators had better go home, keep quiet, and return to their proper allegiance (*vs. 10–12*).

Within this framework the psalmist puts into the king's mouth words that came to have a Messianic meaning. The authority of the new king is grounded in the fact that God has made him a "son of God" at his coronation.

Now we do not, of course, say that Jesus at his ascension was made God's Son. We affirm that he always was God's Son. But we do say that he is, at the ascension, recognizable as God's Son, or as the world's King. And most certainly we say that his enthronement brings to an end an era of defeat and doubt. The old incompetent king, whose death inspired the psalm, is seen as the devil, the lord of darkness, whose reign is ended for all those who accept the message of the ascension.

PSALM 110

The other psalm with special "Messianic" associations—more celebrated, indeed, than Ps. 2—is *Ps. 110*. Few psalms are quoted more frequently in the New

Testament or by the early church fathers. (Some of the New Testament references to *v. 1* are Matt. 22:44; 26:64; I Cor. 15:25; Eph. 1:20; Col. 3:1; Heb. 1:13; 8:1; 10:12–13; I Peter 3:22; some references to *v. 4* are Heb. 5:6; 7:17.)

Christian authorities use *Ps. 110* as a proof text to show how the people of ancient times were waiting for the enthronement of a king whom their kings (for example, David, who was assumed to have written the psalm) would call "Lord" (see, e.g., Acts 2:34). If you do not have to assume that David wrote the psalm (as we do not), then it all makes much better sense, though it loses some of its romance. Its opening simply establishes the divine right not of the king's lord, but of the king himself (the psalmist's lord) to reign. Furthermore, it establishes the divine right of the king to conquer everybody and behave as a primitive conqueror is expected to. Most of the psalm is indeed a somewhat barbarous tribal song, with few of the graces that attract our attention to most of the coronation psalms.

And indeed, what its last verse means remains a mystery that neither scholarship nor imagination can readily penetrate. Taking the text as it stands, all we can say is that almost certainly something has been lost. It almost looks like a reference to Judg. 7:5—but that hardly helps, for what, really, does that innocent-looking passage about Gideon mean? Possibly the "brook" is some sacred fountain with half-superstitious associations; possibly the passage we have lost draws a picture of the king as a traveling conqueror whom God refreshes as he goes.

That we must leave undecided; but the real life of *Ps.*

110 for Christian interpretation is in what it says about the priesthood of the king (*v. 4;* Heb., chs. 7 and 8). The reference to Melchizedek arouses memories of that unforgettable story in Gen., ch. 14, where Melchizedek, "king of Salem," assumes authority to overrule the purposes of the patriarch Abraham. Melchizedek is the first priest mentioned in the Bible, and the context is the first war. The story establishes the ancient principle that a war can be just only if the victor makes no personal gain from it (a principle that Saul notoriously defied, with disastrous results, as we see in I Sam., chs. 16 and 28). Melchizedek, the local king, teaches this truth to Abraham, the destined father of all the faithful. What is more, to ratify the covenant thus entered into, the king of Salem "brought out bread and wine."

This is what makes the psalm worth all the time that Christian expositors have spent on it. For it shows that its real subject is not the divine right of kings in general, but divine right *as Israel saw it;* that is, the right to rule based on the duty of obedience to God. That is the real sense of it. Christian imagination, of course, has also been fascinated by the "bread and wine" covenant of Gen., ch. 14, and has interpreted it thus: "Here, ascended to God's right hand, is our King, who in bread and wine has reminded us of God's authority and love. He is our priest as Melchizedek was to Abraham." Once again, it is an obedience more profound than that which the godliest of earthly kings could achieve, for the true Son of God issues in a power more lasting, more loving, and more assured.

PSALM 27

It is interesting to note that the old liturgies pre-scribe *vs. 1, 7,* and *9* of *Ps. 27* for the Sunday following Ascension Day. In this well-loved psalm there are two parts—*vs. 1–6,* a song of faith, and *vs. 7–14,* a petition for the continuance of God's mercy. The song of faith runs its course confidently and memorably, establishing the connection between regular worship and the disper-sal of anxiety. The second part, which is usually supposed to have a different author, opens with a confession of unworthiness, and an acknowledgment that however badly people treat him, God will look after him, giving him the protection that false parents have denied (*v. 10*) and a fair hearing that false justice has withheld (*v. 12*).

The thought of *v. 10* appears in the very words of our Lord—"Brother will deliver up brother to death, and the father his child" (Matt. 10:21). So does that of *v. 13* of this psalm, when Jesus says, "Truly, I say to you, there is no one who has left house or brothers . . . for my sake and for the gospel, who will not receive a hundredfold now in this time . . ." (Mark 10:29–30).

This gives a clue to the connection between this psalm and the ascension faith. The life of Jesus that preceded the ultimate sacrifice was precisely a matter of trusting in the Father who alone was his light and salvation, when parents and friends deserted him. In the end, God "took him up"—which in one sense means exactly "took him home."

PSALM 23

From this thought we proceed naturally to the most beloved of all the psalms. No one reading Ps. 27 can fail to be reminded of the Twenty-third Psalm, which says almost exactly the same thing, except that the substitution of "shepherd" for "light" provides a significantly different thought.

In *Ps. 23* the psalmist comes right alongside the humblest believer, in whose life, wherever he is, there is loneliness, requiring companionship (*v. 1*); fatigue, requiring refreshment (*v. 2*); error, requiring correction (*v. 3*); terror, requiring reassurance (*v. 4*); stern challenge, requiring fortitude (*v. 5*); and a sense of transitoriness, requiring an assurance of an eternal home (*v. 6*). The believer knows times when he feels like a king (*v. 5*) and times when he feels like a lost child (*v. 4*).

The answer to this is the Shepherd, who, as the teaching of Jesus shows, is a mixture of limitless strength and limitless tenderness. To fetch the lost sheep, the shepherd has a long and dangerous journey. To gather the sheep into his fold, the shepherd must face wolves. (Matt., ch. 18; John, ch. 10.) This is exactly what our Lord did in his redemption. The meanings of *Ps. 23* are endless, its interpretations inexhaustible. We may end with Isaac Watts's comment, added to his metrical version of this psalm:

> There would I find a settled rest,
>   While others go and come;
> No more a stranger or a guest,
>   But like a child at home.

King and child are brought together in the mystery of the ascension, as are the Twenty-third Psalm and Jesus' promise, "In my Father's house are many rooms; . . . I go to prepare a place for you."

9. THE CITY

Psalms 87, 48, 46, 68, 145, 150

The Christian observance of the season of Pentecost leads us to think of the City of God. The psalms that have come to be associated with Pentecost invite us in various ways to consider the glory of that City and the honors of its citizenship. Acts, ch. 2, tells us that the primary thought in the minds of the first Christian preachers was that Christ's work was done; he was risen from death, and now it was possible for all the world, believing this (Acts 2:39), to inherit God's promises. The whole world could now become the City of God.

PSALM 87

"Glorious things of thee are spoken." So, quoting *Ps. 87:3*, begins John Newton's great hymn that expounds this psalm. It is a psalm of joy in citizenship; but, as we have it, it is somewhat fragmentary and confused. A reliable modern commentator suggests that it reads better if a line from *v. 5* is put in after *v. 1*, so that we then read:

> On the holy mount stands the city he founded;
> the Most High himself will establish her.

The opening picture is of the city itself, the historic Jerusalem, standing there in the hills. Surely God must love this place above all others! (*v. 2*). God has indeed spoken a word of special favor to her (*v. 3*). (The speaker here is undoubtedly God.)

To understand the next verses, reread what we said about the pilgrim psalms in Chapter 5. Here again is the procession of people from all over the known world. There are faithful people in Rahab (i.e., Egypt) and Babylon, Philistia and Tyre—all the godless nations and capitals of the pagan world. They come to Jerusalem and one pilgrim says to another, "Where do you come from?" "From Egypt (or, from Babylon), where I was born." Ah, says the psalmist, but in a sense you were all born here; this is your home. (*Vs. 4–5.*)

What would we not give to know the full text of the hymn—obviously a popular one—whose first line is the last line of the psalm, "All my springs are in you" (*v. 7*)! No doubt it was a hymn that spoke of their common citizenship in Jerusalem. Now we worship God not in this or that holy mountain (John 4:20) but wherever in a faithful heart there is a highway to Zion. Exiles in this life can say of the eternal fellowship, "I was born there; I have a citizen's rights there."

PSALM 48

Here is a psalm now associated with Pentecost, and devoted to very much the same subject as Ps. 87. The psalmist sings of God's mercy in preserving the beloved city through so many terrible pages of history (*vs. 1–8*); the remembered hazards make him look the more affectionately at every stone in its walls as the Temple procession winds around its courts (*vs. 12–13*); and he says, with the greatest urgency, "Never let your children forget your history, or the mercy of your God" (*vs. 13–14*).

PSALM 46

The joy of citizenship, expressed in a sense of triumphant security, is the subject of the even more familiar *Ps. 46*. It gave Luther the initial idea for his most famous hymn, "A Mighty Fortress Is Our God." This is one of the Psalter's real folk songs, with its stirring refrain in *vs. 7* and *11*. It is almost an Old Testament version of Paul's magnificent cry of faith in Rom. 8:31: "If God is for us, who is against us?" And the words of the refrain are mysteriously taken up in Isa. 7:14, quoted in Matt. 1:23: " 'Emmanuel' (. . . God with us)." They open up the whole gospel of the Prince of Peace, who ultimately conquers—not by "desolations" (*v. 8*), but because he "makes wars cease" (*v. 9*) by gentleness and love.

The earthly Jerusalem has its imperfections, one of the most conspicuous of which is its scanty water supply. It has no river; its geographical position makes a river impossible. All that it has is an artificial aqueduct (referred to in John 5:2). So the dreams of the celestial city always include a great river (Ezek., ch. 47; Rev., ch. 22), a "river of grace." Thus the image in *v. 4* of a river refreshing Jerusalem passes easily into the Christian idea of the "stream of grace," as in the old hymn, written for Pentecost, which begins:

> Come, thou Fount of every blessing,
>   Tune my heart to sing thy grace;
> Streams of mercy, never ceasing,
>   Call for songs of loudest praise.
>   —*Robert Robinson, 1758*

Thus the gentle and refreshing stream balances the inspiriting but austere pictures of the power of God. Together the power and the blessing are the foundation of the new city.

PSALM 68

And now, in another psalm anciently associated with Pentecost, we come to the most formidable of the psalms in the whole book. For all its obscurity and sternness, *Ps. 68* has built itself into history and doctrine. It was one of the battle songs of the Reformation, and it is the basis of a profound argument about the ascension in Eph., ch. 4—the argument being founded on a reading of the text somewhat different from the one we follow here. This psalm clearly has to do with an act of dramatic worship associated with the covenant festival (Chapter 3), which was also the harvest festival.

Psalm 68 begins with a theophany, an appearance of God as the Lord of Israel before whom enemies withdraw in confusion while the faithful stand fast and rejoice (*vs. 1–3*). At once there follows praise of the acts of God who, as the ideal king (cf. Ps. 72, Chapter 6), reverses the fortunes of all who are oppressed. Then there is a creedal rehearsal (*vs. 7–10*) of God's historic act in the exodus, as is proper to a liturgical psalm (cf. Ps. 114, Chapter 2).

And then we turn to the present, and to a tremendous representation of the powerful Word of God (cf. Ps. 29, Chapter 7). Here is the first verse that suggests Pentecost—"great is the host of those who bore the tidings" (*v. 11*). The enemies of the Word scatter in confusion, and God appears in a devastating brightness. The hills of the battlefield are covered not with corpses but with light, so that they look like snow-covered mountains, the green and gold of the trees blazing out in reflected glory. (*Vs. 11–14*.)

No god is like this living God! The gods who live in the "many-peaked mountain" of Bashan cannot stand before the God who lives in *this* holy hill (that is, Zion, *vs. 15–16*). The triumph of this God is like a victorious procession, with thousands of prisoners following the conqueror, and then, the image dissolving as if handled by a skilled film technician, the procession becomes the procession of joyful worshipers (*vs. 19–20*). Whether they are faithful or rebellious, the king receives tribute from them all (*v. 18*).

The conqueror image comes back, for there are still rebels in the earth (*vs. 21–23*); then the worship image overlays it again, and as the procession draws nearer (*v. 24*) one can distinguish the different choirs, the insignia of the different tribes, the musicians, and the singers (*vs. 25–27*). All of this is in honor of the living God before whom everything must bow (*vs. 28–35*).

This is pure dramatic ecstasy, image following image, idea confused with idea, but the whole picture, so full of energy, is exactly what illustrates the wild power of Pentecost.

Now we must deal with that quotation in Ephesians, which presents something of a problem to the careful reader. In Ephesians, *Ps. 68:18* is quoted as follows:

> When he ascended on high he led
> a host of captives,
> and he gave gifts to men.
> (Eph. 4:8, RSV)

In the text of *Ps. 68* (RSV) this verse reads:

> Thou didst ascend the high mount,
> leading captives in thy train,
> and receiving gifts among men.
> (*Ps. 68:18*, RSV)

The KJV produces one memorable phrase and one incomprehensible one:

> Thou hast ascended on high, thou hast led
> captivity captive:
> Thou hast received gifts for men.
> (*Ps. 68:18*, KJV)

The author of Ephesians interpreted the verse as the KJV did, and thus made it a prophecy of Christ giving men, after the ascension, the gifts of the Spirit. This, which is only a subsidiary argument in the epistle, would clearly seem to be based on a wrong reading of the text in the psalm. We lose little and gain much by the correction and interpretation suggested here and accepted by many scholars, for the value of *Ps. 68* is in the unforgettable impression it leaves of the energy of the Word of God.

PSALM 145

Creative power is the common theme in all the psalms that old liturgies have associated with Pentecost. We have reviewed Ps. 48 and 68 in this chapter, and Ps. 104 in Chapter 7. There remains the wholly peaceful and delightful *Ps. 145*.

This is a song of the Kingdom of God—the world as God's City. It is not in any sense an enthronement psalm, even though it addresses God (*vs. 1–7*) in language appropriate to a royal presence. It is a "variation" psalm, written in acrostic form (see what was said about Ps. 111 in Chapter 3), and it speaks as eloquently to Christians as it did to ancient Israel about the Kingdom of God.

The Kingdom consists of generation following generation (*vs. 1–7*) and telling of the mighty acts of God (cf. the same thought in Ps. 78:2–4). In *v. 8* the singer turns to God's compassion and his nearness to his people. In *vs. 10–13* all creation is called to his praise and to tell of the pleasures of living in the Kingdom. God comes near and establishes his Kingdom of peace, giving his creatures food (*vs. 15–16*), establishing justice (*v. 17*), and answering prayer (*vs. 18–19*). Like a good ruler, he is always and in every way available to his people.

Like Ps. 23, this psalm is immediately understood and loved wherever men sing it. For all her sufferings—perhaps partly because of them—Israel has learned the secret of joy in the presence of God.

PSALM 150

This psalm of universal praise fittingly closes these meditations for the season of Pentecost. *Psalm 150* concludes a short section of five psalms, all of which begin with the word "Hallelujah" (Hebrew for "Praise the Lord"). The first three of them we have already dealt with (Ps. 146 in Chapter 4; Ps. 147 and 148 in Chapter 7). The psalm preceding (Ps. 149) is a war dance that was associated especially with the Maccabean Revolt (beginning in 166 B.C.) and was a favorite song of the suffering peoples of Europe during the Thirty Years' War (1618–1648). It is vengeful, fierce, and appropriate to the trying days of Israel's persecution.

But *Ps. 150* is pure and unalloyed praise. It needs no detailed comment, and we shall say only two things. First, the ecstasy of praise, emerging in dance as well as song (we saw it above in Ps. 68), contrasts sharply and even shamingly with the often meager and inhibited gestures that pass for praise among modern Christians. The Israelites, from the days of the primitive prophets (I Sam. 10:5; and see especially II Sam. 6:14), praised God with their bodies; they gave the whole man to praise. The "dance" (*v. 4*) has disappeared from worship, but has anything taken its place to symbolize the total self-giving of praise?

Secondly, as to "Let everything that breathes praise the LORD!" (*v. 6*), "breath" and "spirit" are the same word in Hebrew, in Greek, and in Latin. It is with the life that God has given us (Ps. 104:30) that we praise. It is with the renewed life of the Spirit that we praise in

Christ. Praise is a full circle, beginning and ending with God. The circuit can be broken only by man's rebellion and forgetfulness. This is the final lesson of Pentecost.

10. FAITH

Psalms 95, 82, 19, 119, 90, 91, 77

Traditional liturgy recognizes what is called "Trinity Sunday" as the beginning of the second half of the church year. Tradition further dictates that this part of the year shall be given to teaching about the faith that has been dramatically set forth in the first half (culminating in Pentecost). This suggests that we now consider certain psalms that express Israel's understanding of the faith and that lead into the Christian understanding.

PSALM 95

Psalm 95 illustrates very well the threefold structure of Israel's historic faith: belief in God the Creator; belief in God the historic Redeemer; and moral responsibility arising from these beliefs.

The psalm is in two clearly defined parts, of which the first (*vs. 1–7*) is given to the first of these three articles of faith. The Creator God is the ground of Israel's faith—the ground of its very being. God is the Maker (*vs. 3–5*) and the Shepherd (*vs. 6–7a*); therefore, the people are called to worship him.

In the second part (*vs. 7b–11*), the psalm turns to the theme of redemption, which historically is the theme of the exodus. It is, in fact, the work of God toward Israel that identifies him in the people's faith, and not merely an abstract idea of a divine creator. In *v. 7* we have already seen him spoken of as the people's shepherd. At once the psalmist extracts a moral: first from the "testing" of Massah and Meribah (Ex. 17:7; cf. Ps. 81, Chapter 3), in which the people's lack of trust in God was proved to them, and God's mercy vindicated; then by reference to the belief that the duration of that long journey (forty years from Egypt to Palestine is, even by ancient standards, slow-moving) was directly due to the people's obstinate disobedience (see Deut. 3:23–27). The fulfillment of the promise of Canaan was not for any deserving of Israel, but in spite of their disobedience. Hence the threatening note on which the psalm closes (commented on profoundly in Heb. 3:7–19 and 4:3–11), and the central exhortation, "O that today you would hearken to his voice!"

PSALM 82

"You shall have no other gods before me"—so runs the First Commandment, the basis of all Israel's morality. *Psalm 82* is a dramatic presentation of that truth. The kernel of disobedience and unfaithfulness is always, for Israel, idolatry. So their songs of faith are full of denunciations of the "gods of the heathen" (cf. Ps. 115, Chapter 2).

In *Ps. 82* we have a magnificent flight of poetic imagination. All the heathen deities are on trial, and the living God is judging them (*v. 1*). The indictment is threefold: Their justice is illusory (*vs. 2–4*); their worship leads to blindness and confusion (*v. 5*); and they have no immortality, no authority that men do not have (*vs. 6–7*). The last verse points the moral: There is but one God, and the world must serve him.

The point here is that all gods are nothing but projections of human notions (but not so the living God!). Man may call them gods, but they are as mortal as men (*v. 7*). There is nothing objective about them— therefore, no principle of immutable justice; they say what men tell them to say.

Put all the idols and false values of the modern world up there along with Molech and Venus, and let the living God judge them and expel them with the rest of the company of false arbiters of life.

PSALM 19

The splendor of *Ps. 19* is, like that of Ps. 27, partly the result of inspired editing. Two psalms have been joined together; but once joined, let no man put them asunder! Here is Ps. 95 over again, but in what to an Israelite of our Lord's time would be a "modern" form. We begin, as in the older psalm, with the creation—the word of God in nature. "The heavens are telling the glory of God." Immediately the psalmist introduces a fascinating and highly original picture. Day and night (*v. 2*), standing for the whole of nature, are the record of God's grandeur and love. There is no audible speech, yet their voice is heard everywhere. Similarly the sun (*vs. 4b–6*), the greatest visible glory, reflects God's faithfulness in the rhythm of its apparent movements. The gaiety and dignity of this passage are unexampled in literature— powerful even by the standards of the Psalter.

Then the singer, directed by this inspired editor, turns at once to the word of God that comes from within: the reviving law, the enlightening testimony (*v. 7*); the just precepts, the righteous commandments (*v. 8*); the cleansing fear, the trustworthy ordinances (*v. 9*); all is summed up in a verse of praise (*v. 10*) and a prayer for obedience (*vs. 12–14*). This is faith—the word within responding to the word from eternity.

A most important point emerges here: to the faithful Israelite "the law" was never a dead thing, whatever later legalism made of it. It was honored not in blind obedience but in right decisions. In Deut. 5:3 there is a text that drives this truth home: "Not with our fathers did the LORD make this covenant, but with us, who are all of us here alive this day."

PSALM 119

We must therefore turn at once to that astonishing literary tour de force, *Ps. 119*, of which Ps. 19:7–10 gives us a brief foretaste. It must firmly be said that *Ps. 119*, for all its length, is not the tedious and repetitive self-advertising document that some people have supposed it to be. It is a celebration of the living law.

Each verse in an eight-verse section is built around a word (a different word each time within the section) that is a synonym for the word of God. Without going into minute detail (requiring too much length of exposition for this study), we shall simply say that in the original version of the psalm each section used one of eight words for the "law" once only. (In the RSV there are actually thirteen synonyms, irregularly used: e.g., "law" appears twenty-five times; "word," twenty-three times; "statutes" and "commandment(s)," twenty-two times each; "surety," "appointment," and "faithfulness," only once each.)

This hardly matters much. If the other acrostic psalms are "variations on a theme," this one is like a *passacaglia*—having a constant ground bass. Within this framework—and we may add that this is the only psalm which actually *rhymes* in the original Hebrew—the psalmist explores every possible situation in life in which obedience to the law of God is put to the test: persecution, false accusation, inner temptation, rational argument. These and a score of other situations are mentioned; and now and again the author comes out with some triumphant statements of faith like that in *v. 96:*

> I have seen a limit to all perfection,
>   but thy commandment is exceedingly broad.

All the phrases in Ps. 19:7–10 are repeated here or there in *Ps. 119;* and the sum of it is in the beautiful last verse:

> I have gone astray like a lost sheep; seek
>   thy servant,
>   for I do not forget thy commandments.

PSALM 90

This, one of the most solemn of the psalms, is the basis of Isaac Watts's most famous hymn, "Our God, Our Help in Ages Past." Here faith explores the implications of God's eternity as contrasted with man's transitoriness.

Imagination is kindled by its heading, "A Prayer of Moses, the man of God." And although we must treat that heading with the same reserve with which we approach all traditional historical statements about the psalms, we might at least say that there is more of the viewpoint of the Pentateuch here than anywhere else in the Psalter.

After the famous opening line, which sets the tone of faith, we proceed at once to the Creation (v. 2), and then to the problem of death (vs. 3–6). This establishes the metaphysical distinction between God and man—God alone cannot die. But then, in a characteristically Old Testament way, metaphysics gives way to morals. (So it is when we pass from ch. 1 to ch. 2 of Genesis.) God is eternal, but also perfect; man's mortality is linked with man's imperfection. Man must then pray for "wisdom" that will enable him to understand this and accept it humbly (vs. 11–12).

What hope, then, can be found? The answer is an urgent appeal (v. 13) to God's known and demonstrated grace. God can "return" and give happiness, overruling and directing man's work (vs. 13–17).

It is this sense of utter helplessness in the face of death, and of irrevocable sin, that sets the scene for the drama of our redemption in Christ. Christ is the world's only hope—let the quacks and horoscope purveyors and tranquilizer merchants do what they will. (See Mark 5:26 for an exact personal picture of a woman's helplessness in the face of death!)

PSALM 91

In a more personal—if less profound—fashion, *Ps. 91* pursues the thought with which Ps. 90 opened. *Psalm 91* is a dramatic conversation. The first two verses state the opening theme. There is a delightful picture in the word "abides" in *v. 1;* it means "lodges" or "stays the night." Then the voice of a friend comes in, addressing the man of faith, and this continues through *v. 13.* God will defend the faithful man from life's hazards (*vs. 3–6*), covering him "like an eagle . . . that flutters over its young" (Deut. 32:11).

Finally the voice of God is heard (*vs. 14–16*), and this is the heart of the matter: "Because he cleaves to me in love, I will deliver him."

Verses 11–12 have become especially hallowed for Christians by their use in the story of our Lord's temptations (Matt. 4:6; Luke 4:11). Our Lord's use of the psalm (the account of his temptations must necessarily have come from his own lips) shows us that to treat the psalm as an arrogant assumption of special providences deserved by righteousness is, precisely, the devil's work. There are passages, such as *vs. 7–8*, that lend themselves to that interpretation. But we must resist the temptation, and interpret this, as all Old Testament Scripture, in the light of the New Testament. It is faith that brings a sense of safety—not human virtue or human good fortune that claims to deserve it.

PSALM 77

How the faith, especially the redemptive faith, affects a man's personal life is well illustrated in *Ps. 77*. Like the author of Ps. 22 (see Chapter 1), the writer is remembering a time of serious illness, or perhaps of grievous mental anguish, which has been enough to make him wonder whether God has not altogether deserted him (*vs. 7–9*). He finds comfort for his sorrow in telling himself again the story of God's redemption of Israel—the story of the exodus, when men saw that God's "way was through the sea." He applies the objective historical faith to his own condition, and his pain is eased. (*Vs. 11–19*.)

Between these two sections there is a baffling and tantalizing verse, of which even the RSV does not make much sense—*v. 10*. There is a tiresome textual difficulty here. The RSV reads:

> And I say, "It is my grief
>   that the right hand of the Most High
>   has changed."

The KJV has a much more attractive rendering:

> And I said, This is my infirmity:
> But I will remember the years of the right hand
>   of the Most High.

Yet another translation is given by Briggs in The International Critical Commentary:

> Then I said, I will begin with this: the years of the right
> hand of the Most High.

The trouble is that there are two words in the
Hebrew whose meaning is quite uncertain, the one
translated either "my grief" or "I will begin," and the
other translated "the years" or "has changed." There is
doubt also about the word behind "I will remember."
We must regretfully dismiss the KJV as being a little
too speculative. The RSV leaves us with the sense: "The
real origin of my sorrow is my thought that God has
changed (i.e., deserted me), but I was wrong." Briggs's
rendering gives the sense: "I will dismiss all my own
thoughts, and begin over again with the fundamental of
my faith." Whatever is right, it is clear what the sense
requires: a contrast between the loneliness of pain,
which can be a self-sought loneliness, and the power of
the objective facts to dispel it. Thinking what God has
done for others among your own people can effectively
heal the sense of desolation that pain can bring; at least,
that is practical faith.

11. LIFE'S STRESS

Psalms 11, 55, 62, 141, 4, 13, 137, 80

Let us now consider some of the psalms that tell of the application of faith to the hazards and stresses that life brings to every man. First we shall look at three psalms that mention failures in friendship and then at a variety of others that arise from such troubles as anxiety, strife, loneliness, and grief.

PSALM 11

The Book of Job, of which the Psalter so constantly reminds us, is largely an account of a conversation between Job and three friends who show a well-meant misunderstanding of both his condition and his moral quality. Something of the kind must be behind *Ps. 11*, which seems to begin, as it were, at the end of such a conversation. Here is a man, hard pressed by the difficulties of life, to whom some well-meaning person has said, "Flee like a bird to the mountains" (or possibly, "You birds, flee to the mountains," quoting some proverb). People who seek to be sympathetic often say, "Why not get away from it all?" without realizing that their counsel could be taken as an encouragement to cowardice. "Look," say the friends, "you can't possibly win."

The psalmist replies: "On the contrary, I can. I have put my trust in God." And then he goes on (*vs. 4–7*) to declare his faith in the God who will justify him against those who are seeking his downfall. This is a simple piece of rugged, everyday heroism. The one thing that undermines a man's morale more surely than anything else is moral fatigue, weariness, the temptation to give up the struggle. A man moral enough to have entered on the struggle in the first place will not be helped by enticements to escape; if he gets out, he will be unable to live with himself anyway.

PSALM 55

Exactly the same thought is in the longer and more poignant *Ps. 55*. This is much more highly charged with emotion, less rugged and sturdy, than Ps. 11. The psalmist is in real trouble: Enemies press on him from every side; worries, anxieties, frustrations, misfortunes, call them what you will, are the most real things he can see at the moment. Indeed, he is tempted to fly away on a bird's wings and be at rest. (*Vs. 6–8*.) It is a sorry business indeed when the wilderness seems to afford more consolation than the city where his friends live.

But that is the worst of it: "It is not an enemy who taunts me—then I could bear it; . . . but it is you, . . . my familiar friend" (*vs. 12–14, 20–21*). One whom he thought he could trust has betrayed him—one with whom he went to worship has let him down. That is the depth out of which he cries to the Lord, and when he is in the grip of despair, immortal words form themselves in his mind, "Cast your burden on the LORD" (*v. 22*).

This psalm, like many of its kind, is a disconcerting alternation of imprecation and pious prayer. It is none the worse for this; life is, in fact, like that. But another text comes to mind, one we have quoted before: "A man's foes will be those of his own household" (Matt. 10:36). Let us take this one step farther—what if the close and trusted friend from whom for years he has been inseparable is himself? The tragedy is at its greatest then, and a man may well curse himself as he has cursed his enemy.

Once again, however, though tempted to run away, he has faced the hazards of life in complete trust that, whatever friends may betray him, God will never turn away a man who comes to him with a burden.

PSALM 62

Here is a third psalm that may well have come out of the experience of treachery. It is in some ways reminiscent of Ps. 42 and 43; like those psalms (taken together), this has a two-verse refrain which interrupts its lamentation, and seems to provide a foothold which the sufferer cannot always find.

There is much in *Ps. 62* about enemies. The special character of these enemies is revealed in *v. 4:* "They bless with their mouths, but inwardly they curse." The reference this time is not precisely to a lifelong friend who suddenly reveals unsuspected depths of treachery, but to the two-faced bonhomie of the morally dishonest.

Indeed, this could easily be the song of a modern businessman who has fallen among thieves. They conspire to do him in (*v. 3*), to make him "like a leaning wall, a tottering fence."

One thing he has learned—that the world's evaluations of men are illusory (*v. 9*); that "high" and "low," eminent or obscure, according to public values, are so much nonsense. And if anybody wants his advice, it is this (*v. 10*): any man who builds hopes on worldly wealth, and who will do anything to get it, will find out before he dies how barren his hopes were.

All this the psalmist has learned. He puts down his own experience dramatically, but he has already come through it. He has learned to wait for God in silence (*vs. 1, 5*), to regard God as his rock and his refuge (*v. 7*). Not once only, but constantly in his worship he has heard that power belongs not to the worldly successes, but "to God" (*v. 11*). Out of his experience he exhorts all who will hear to trust in God, and to be silent before him (cf. Ps. 46:10).

PSALM 141:1–5

This concept of silence before God is central to Old Testament religion, and it is a central truth of human life. If men will only listen! How much confusion and grief would be avoided if men were less ready to speak, less insistent on having the last word! There is a beautiful fragment in *Ps. 141*, whose text is so hopelessly confused that only five verses of it make any sense at all, but those five verses are precious. They are an evening prayer (*v. 2*) such as a man might make in his house; and in his prayer he is praying for the golden gift of silence. "Set a guard over my mouth, O LORD," he says (*v. 3*); one becomes talkative and careless in speech through many temptations, especially the temptation to be liked by the influential and to make an impression on the powerful. In such company, the tongue's purity is the first casualty (*v. 4*). Rather, the psalmist prays that he may learn to listen even to words of rebuke from upright men; it is better to be criticized by the wise than praised by the wicked, even when their praise is as fragrant and refreshing as oil (*v. 5*). Two thirds of the way through *v. 5* the psalm falls into confusion. The RSV does its best, but the reader need not concern himself with so dubious a reconstruction of a text whose original form we do not know. Staying with what is clear, he does better to recall the words of The Letter of James about the unruly tongue (James 3:1–12), and those of our Lord about accepting suffering and rebuke, from whatever hand, rather than inflicting it ourselves (Matt. 5:38–42).

PSALM 4

This is another psalm of peace, uttered by a man who knows the world's strife. Again (*v. 8*) it seems to be a domestic evening prayer, and again it is a prayer for the gift of silence (*v. 4*). Like all men of piety, he knows what it is to have people scoff at his faith. He sounds like a man who has to work alongside unbelievers, whose values are "vain words and . . . lies" (*v. 2*)—and what faithful Christian has not known that experience? (If he has not suffered for it, perhaps he has never witnessed

at all for his faith.) He declares his own faith, and
recommends to others what he asks for himself, that
they "tremble and sin not," and that they "be silent."
(The former phrase is suggested as a better reading for
v. 4. The translation in the RSV is tempting because it
seems to be taken up in Eph. 4:26; but once again, if our
view is correct, the apostle has referred in passing to a
doubtful text. See the material in Chapter 9 on Ps. 68.)

The psalmist invites his unbelieving colleagues to try
going to church (*v. 5*). If people all around him are
wanting to know where to find goodness (*v. 6*), let them
know that, for his own part, God gives him more joy
than the joy of a good harvest (*v. 7*)—which is not far
from saying, as a man might say in a modern discussion
with his workmates, more joy than a million dollars.
Finally, he turns to God in trust and lies down to sleep
(*v. 8*).

PSALM 13

The authors of Ps. 141 and 4, which we have just
read, are poets who have found the secret of peace. But
not all the psalmists see things in the same way. Some
of their utterances are darker and more strained. *Psalm
13* is perhaps the simplest of all the psalms of suffering;
its pattern is one we have encountered many times
before. An experience of desolation (*vs. 1–4*) is set
alongside a statement of religious faith (*vs. 5–6*), without comment. There is no diagnosis or prescription, as in
Ps. 77. It is more like a miniature Ps. 22. It would appear
that the source of the psalmist's grief and sense of
dereliction here is again personal—it is the people he

meets who make life almost unlivable. It is personal
relations that generate the most piercing pains and the
most immediate pleasures. But what of his relation with
God? Is this broken? How long must he be uncertain?
Perhaps remembering when this was his condition
before, and how God delivered him, he records his
thanksgiving for what he expects of God now.

PSALM 137

We passed lightly over Ps. 13, which, to be sure, adds
hardly anything to what we have said in earlier chapters, but it does provide an introduction to a psalm that
is at the same time one of the most beautiful and one of
the most notorious—*Ps. 137.*

The thing that most people remember about *Ps. 137* is
the appalling imprecation in its last verse; but the
keynote of the psalm is not anger, but grief.

It comes from a historical situation, of course, which,
almost uniquely in the Psalter, is identifiable. It is a
song of the Babylonian exile, when all the people of any
distinction and influence in Jerusalem had been de-
ported after the disaster of 586 B.C. (A glance back at
the introduction to Chapter 5 will remind the reader
what this meant.) These people were literally cut off
from all contact with their God. They had only recently
come to believe that their meeting place with God was
Jerusalem, and only Jerusalem. Now they were impossibly far away. It is a religious homesickness for which
Christian experience (thanks to the blessed miracle of
the ascension and Pentecost) knows no parallel.

So here is this musician, who has dragged his instrument (not, by the way, a harp such as we are familiar with now, but something much more like a guitar) away from the ruined city, and who is now taunted by his captors, who say, "Play us one of your tunes." It is this musician who says, "May my right hand be paralyzed and may I never sing another note, if I forget my beloved city!" To remember—to keep alive the memory —is all he can do now. No wonder that he turns with terrible words on his captors and utters things that seem almost beyond forgiveness.

In reading this poignant document, we must (1) put far from our minds the thought that we are too enlightened to say anything like *vs. 7–9;* (2) wonder in penitence whether any part of our own religion would move us to say anything like *vs. 1–6;* and (3) remember that the enemies of the New Jerusalem may be those of her own household.

PSALM 80

Occasions when Jerusalem fell to invaders and suffered indignities have often been referred to in psalms we have already considered. *Psalm 80* is probably a very primitive psalm that enshrines a public lament at the destruction of some city—possibly Samaria, which fell in 722 B.C., or possibly a lesser place of hallowed association. The general drift is quite clear. It is a song with a refrain for congregational use; it has much of the primitive dignity of Ps. 90.

Psalm 80 gives voice to the people's constant question in times of trouble, "Why did God bring us out of Egypt, only to allow us to be destroyed and persecuted here?"

(as *vs. 8–13* might be summarized). The psalm itself issues in a repeated prayer that God will yet rescue the people. But it is unusual in referring to Israel as "a vine." Two other passages in Scripture interpret it, the second bringing it directly within a New Testament understanding.

It is suggested that the reader first turn to Ezek., ch. 15, in which Jerusalem is denounced as being an unfruitful vine. The point is there made that the vine is a plant with one special property. If it fails in bearing grapes, it is useless for anything else. Ezekiel says that you cannot make even a peg out of it. Let the vine do its work (of proclaiming and living out the faith committed to it). And then one's finger goes irresistibly to the fifteenth chapter of John, where our Lord says exactly the same thing of his disciples. The unprofitable branch, i.e., the disciple who does not abide in Christ, who is not obedient to his word, falls away from the vine, spent and useless. For Christ is the principle of the vine, its life, its purpose. "For apart from me you can do nothing." (John 15:5.)

12. WISDOM

Psalms 73, 37, 39, 49, 107

We come now to a group of psalms that in various ways seek to explore the secrets of life. The wise man, in the view that prevailed in Old Testament times, is the man who can refer the problems of life to his faith, who can close the gap between faith and everyday life—the man who neither thinks so "spiritually" as to be unrealistic nor is so committed to worldly values as to ignore the rebuke that faith offers to those values.

PSALM 73

People have not yet stopped asking, "Why does a loving God permit evil?" They were, as *Ps. 73* shows us, asking it in Old Testament days. Once again we must recall The Book of Job, which is devoted to that question. This psalm is the statement of a man who has found an answer that none can gainsay. He begins with a declaration of faith. "Truly God is good to the upright" (possibly, "to Israel"). He was taught this when he was young. Experience tempted him to doubt it. Faith has at last confirmed it.

When he was young (*v. 2*) he knew what it was to wonder, in an envious way, why the "arrogant" so often seemed to succeed in the world. He proceeds to describe the self-indulgence (*v. 7*), the scorn (*v. 8*), the godless profanity (*v. 9*) of the unscrupulous, and their astounding immunity from heavenly judgment (*v. 5*); they seem to get away with anything. They become well known and respected (*v. 10*), and they openly assume that God will not touch them—that indeed there is no God (*v. 11*). What is the good of keeping one's hands clean when all success seems to go to this kind of person (*vs. 13–14*)? All the thanks one gets is poverty—the honest man's money goes into the dishonest man's pockets.

So the inquirer turns to the house of God. Understanding this vexatious mystery was "a wearisome task" (*v. 16*) until he did so. Two things followed: First, he saw that it was not really true that the impious were immune from judgment. They are strangely vulnerable; one false step, and they are finished. One public scandal, and their names are not mentioned again. (*Vs. 17–20.*) It has happened, perhaps, to people he himself knows. Life is not so irrationally unjust as in moments of grievance we say it is. But secondly, he sees that his depression and pessimism were sinful as well as ill-informed. The glory that surrounds him in the community of faith rebukes his pessimism, showing it to be in itself a self-indulgence. (*Vs. 21–23.*) Of course, he is with God! Of course, God is good!

> Whom have I in heaven but thee?
>> And there is nothing upon earth that I desire
>> besides thee.

My flesh and my heart may fail,
    but God is the strength of my heart and my
        portion for ever.

(*Vs. 25–26*)

This, then, the normal practice of religion, corrects a man's hasty despairs and restores the equilibrium of his mind.

PSALM *37*

The other psalm on the same theme, *Ps. 37*, is an extraordinary document. It is as artificial as Ps. 73 is spontaneous. Like Ps. 111 (see Chapter 3), it is an acrostic, so we can expect some degree of artificiality. And we get it. The whole psalm is a collection of proverbs. It reads like a chapter from the book of Proverbs itself, except that it keeps to the point a little more systematically than Proverbs usually does. The aphorisms are carefully enough collected; but they are, one feels, the memorable statements of somebody who, for all one knows, has never been in business.

The compiler of this psalm was a man well on in years (*v. 25*), and he lays down the law as such a one might to a young nephew or apprentice. He is capable of saying that he has, in all his life, never seen "the godly one forsaken, or his children begging bread" (*v. 25*)—manifestly an oversimplification, if not a downright falsehood. The answer to the problem of evil for him is a series of exhortations to believe in God's justice (*vs. 9–17*), to cultivate contentment and good works (*vs. 3–7*), and not to be too sure that the wicked man will always prosper (*vs. 28–36*).

Now what can be said for this psalm is this: It is a very reasonable way for an old man to talk to a young one. If the youngster has as yet no experience of life, he must accept the word of another, and a good teacher is not above oversimplifying. This teacher insists all the way on the necessity—and indeed on the rewards—of leading a godly life (vs. 37–40). And as a matter of fact, the psalm has an exalted Christian history; v. 11 becomes, in Matt. 5:5, the third Beatitude; v. 5 is the origin of Paul Gerhardt's great hymn (in translation, "Commit Thou All Thy Griefs"); and in v. 7 we have the classic command, "Be still." (See Ps. 62 and comments in Chapter 11.) This is teaching of the kind that became very common in the later days of Israel's literature, and the twenty sayings in this psalm are full of wisdom in capsule form that will do its work for the young man to whom it is addressed.

PSALM 39

Now we may turn to another profound problem, that of death. We have met it before (Ps. 90, Chapter 10). But the most passionate encounter with it is in Ps. 39.

This is a conversation between the poet and God. Boldly and candidly, the poet asks God what can be the meaning of death. He has tried to "be still," to cultivate the gift of silence, but on this point God has said nothing to him. (Vs. 1–3.) So he speaks up—and the rest of the psalm is what he says. There is no answer, except a line in v. 7, "My hope is in thee."

This man, like other Israelites of his time, had no doctrine of an afterlife. God had not yet spoken to Israel on this matter, as he ultimately did in the resurrection of Jesus Christ. For the psalmist, death was seen as simply the gateway to "Sheol," the place where disembodied spirits went, where there was no life or speech, the abode of nothingness. So what could death be but a punishment? The withdrawal of life, and with it all human grace, a mere corruption and waste—that was death. Punishment for what? Why must all humanity be under this sentence of annihilation?

There is no answer yet. The psalm is simply a human document, the record of a wise man's audacious question.

PSALM 49

If the psalmists could not know how to answer the question of death, they could speak about life in relation to death. This is what is done in *Ps. 49*, a psalm that stands, as it were, halfway between the desperate questioning of Ps. 39 and the confidence of Ps. 73. It is concerned with the specific social problem of possession.

The psalmist opens by addressing his song to the rich and the poor (*vs. 1–4*). He himself is a man of no wealth, but he has learned not to be alarmed by the apparent success of the prosperous. It has been abundantly proved that a man who trusts in wealth builds on sand, for life is more than possessions. (*Vs. 7–9.*) Nobody can buy his way out of death (*vs. 10–12*). No man can carry his wealth past the gate of death (*vs. 17–19*). Therefore, the conclusion is, in the refrain in which the listeners perhaps join:

> Man cannot abide in his pomp,
>   he is like the beasts that perish.
>   (*Vs. 12, 20*)

In a sense, this is a positive way of looking at death, for it is an urgent reminder that the power of God is greater than the power that the greatest wealth can give a man. It is therefore an incitement to humility. A man may admit ignorance about the real meaning of death—as the psalmists did—but still be entirely confident that God, with whom is the disposal of death and life, will not allow men, because of their wealth or because of their poverty, to fall outside the field of his justice.

"Truly no man can ransom himself" (*v. 7*)—that is the secret. It was at that point that God could say, in his own good time, "No, *but I can ransom you.*"

PSALM 107

We have seen the limitations of Israel's wisdom, when read by itself and without the benefit of the New Testament. Of what wisdom, then, is it said, "Whoever is wise, let him give heed to these things"?

Those are the closing words of the long, lyrical, and heartening *Ps. 107*. Wisdom may stumble when it tries to handle the future, but it can deal with the past with a sure touch. *Psalm 107* is a mighty, rhythmical thanksgiving for God's providence, and for God's special grace in gathering Israel into a nation.

After a brief introduction (*vs. 1–3*), there are four distinct sections of thanksgiving, and then an epilogue. In the first section (*vs. 4–9*), the ground of thanksgiving is the redemption in the exodus. Arising out of this, three groups of people are then addressed, or the nation is addressed under three figures. These groups are prisoners who had been set free (*vs. 10–16*), sick people who had regained health (*vs. 17–22*), and sailors who had been kept safe (*vs. 23–32*). One can take these as literal conditions for which gratitude was to be shown, or as types of spiritual conditions in which the people at different times had found themselves.

The epilogue (*vs. 33–43*) describes the happy state of things toward which these historical deliverances have led—the establishment of a settled nation, the cultivation of the land and reclamation of the desert, and the satisfactions of the life to which, through the redemption of the exodus, the people were led.

And so, "Whoever is wise, let him give heed to these things; let men consider the steadfast love of the Lord." Here, anyhow, we are on firm ground. It is like the second half of Ps. 77, but communally expressed. Consider what God has done—that is the Hebrew application of creed to life. Take your cue for the future from the past. Israel's faith found its discipline, its limitations, and its triumph within this framework. It was a faith assured of its past, and assured of the promises for the nation, but without assurance for any individual's personal future. The Christian assurance has often been turned into an excuse for shameful negligence of the holy task of the community; from this negligence Israel was delivered. By the same token, Christians are often so preoccupied with personal survival, as a subject in itself, that they think little of that "steadfast love" of God in which Israel had its only hope. Where Christians can rise to the supreme wisdom of Ps. 90, or of this one,

or of Ps. 136, which presents an endless rhythm of
thanksgiving for the one thing that man can count on,
the "steadfast love" of God, then Christians can build
their resurrection faith on such humility and wisdom as
this, and they are wise. If they cannot, their wisdom is
inferior to that of these faithful ancients, for true
wisdom is born of trust in God's steadfast love.

13. CHARACTER

Psalms 1, 24a, 26, 15, 112, 143, 51

In this final study we shall consider a group of psalms that show us what, in the view of the religious Israelite, constituted human goodness. This group falls into two subsections, the first of which comprises four psalms that give positive advice and exhortation about human character. Our study takes us first of all to the beginning of the Psalter as its editors arranged it.

PSALM 1

The First Psalm is usually thought to be a late composition, put into the Psalter as a kind of introduction. It is of interest that in the one place in the New Testament where a psalm is quoted by number (Acts 13:33), what we know as the Second Psalm is referred to, in some ancient manuscripts, as the First Psalm.

Psalm 1 is a very simple statement about the principle of happiness. The good man, it says, avoids the company and the example of those who scornfully defy the law of God; he constantly meditates on the law (*vs.*

1–2). In consequence he will flourish (*v. 3*), but the ungodly will wither (*v. 4*).

The good life, then, is keeping close to God's commandments, and keeping clear of all scandal. It will be rewarded, and there is no compromise possible between the good and the evil.

PSALM 24:1–6

So far, then, everything is very clear. One of the points brought out in *Ps. 24* is the close connection between regular worship and the good life. The first half of this psalm has a passage that mentions this principle. *Psalm 24* is a congregational and dramatic song (the last verses we dealt with in Chapter 8); it opens, therefore, with a spacious statement of God's creative power. But at once it proceeds to a brief sketch of the man who is fit to come to "the hill of the LORD" (that is, to the Temple for worship). This man, who knows the secret of happiness and moral security (*vs. 4–5*), has "clean hands and a pure heart," and "does not lift up his soul to what is false." Rectitude in all dealings is his outstanding quality.

To any who think this a somewhat defective analysis of the goodness that makes a man fit for God's presence, we must point out that, in the days of Israel's faith, common honesty in business was very much less an assumption, guarded by law, than it is in modern Western countries. Even today the idea that a piece of goods has a fair and objective price, independent of personal bargaining, is quite foreign to the Levantine street trader—as many a tourist has learned to his cost. Despite all that is said in the Pentateuch on the subject, the temptation to drive a hard, rather than an honest, bargain (in Luke 16:1–12 this is not regarded as an action too shocking to illustrate a divine truth) was more pressing and more commonly accepted then than it is even now. Nowadays dishonesty is at least recognized for what it is, even where it is practiced without punishment. It was profoundly difficult, in what was in so many ways a very free society, to have "clean hands."

PSALM 26

The cleanhanded man, says Ps. 24, is the man fit for worship. Another psalm, *Ps. 26*, puts it the other way round and says that worship will help a man to keep his hands clean. *Psalm 26* is a kind of amplification of Ps. 1:4–7. It is the song of a man who has to spend much time and energy, and forgo much opportunity of gain, in order to keep clear of dishonesty (*vs. 4–5*). Going to worship to remind himself of the love of God (*vs. 1–3, 6–7*), he prays especially that God will help him to live a good life in a world that makes it intolerably difficult (*vs. 8–12*). In the faith he finds that his "foot stands on level ground." This, then, is the converse of Ps. 24:3–4.

PSALM 15

But the most detailed picture of the good character is in the magnificent *Ps. 15*, which opens with the same question that we encountered in Ps. 24:3. This is indeed worth prolonged meditation. Who, it asks, can come to

worship without a sense of overwhelming shame? First
—the honest man, who deals and speaks without guile
(*v. 2;* cf. Matt. 5:37, "Let what you say be simply 'Yes' or
'No'; anything more than this comes from evil").

Second—the kindly-spoken man. "Take up a reproach
against" means simply "abuse" (*v. 3;* cf. I Cor. 13:4,
"Love is not . . . boastful . . . or rude").

Third—the man who keeps clear of second-rate
morality and honors goodness (*v. 4*): "[Love] does not
rejoice at wrong, but rejoices in the right" (I Cor. 13:6).

Fourth—the faithful man, who, in the version used in
the Anglican Book of Common Prayer, "sweareth unto
his neighbor, and disappointeth him not, though it were
to his own hindrance."

Fifth—the generous man, who will have nothing to
do with usury.

Sixth—the incorruptible man, who will never take a
bribe (*v. 5*). This is the man whose foot "stands on level
ground," as Ps. 26:12 puts it.

Little in this needs any explanation, except perhaps
the prohibition of usury, which to our modern minds is
"interest." Usury is outlawed in Israel; it is part of
normal business life with us. Indeed, our Lord had no
objection to it (see the parable of the talents, Matt.
25:27). The explanation is simple. In a primitive society
the only context in which interest would be gathered
was in personal moneylending. That society depended
on neighborliness rather than on economic law. The
goodwill that would lend money to help a neighbor was
far more important to it than the availability of money
for organized commercial public enterprises, of which
primitive society knew nothing in any modern sense.

Interest is now regarded as a legitimate reward for the risk taken by a man who places money at the disposal of people whom he does not know personally at all. That is the difference. In *Ps. 15* the man who avoids usury is simply the man who is never greedy but is by nature generous. With that morsel of interpretation, *Ps. 15* stands as the best brief account of the good life that has ever been put together.

PSALM 112

Psalm 112, expanding Ps. 1:3, is another description of the good man and of the reward he can expect. It dwells mostly on the point about positive generosity that is made in Ps. 15:5. It is a psalm of praise, beginning, like Ps. 146 to 150, with "Hallelujah," and no doubt was often sung by a large company of people. The good man, it says, delights in God's commandments (*v. 1;* cf. Ps. 1:2), and his reward shall be an abundance of descendants, always a typical blessing for the family-minded Jews (*v. 2;* cf. Ps. 127; 128), prosperity in earthly things (*v. 3*), and a good conscience (*v. 4*).

The secret of this good life is generosity—being as generous as the Lord is (*vs. 4–5*). In particular, the good man will always "lend"—that is, he will use his wealth for purposes out of which he has nothing personal to gain (this is the real spirit of Ps. 15:5). And he will give to anybody who is in need (*v. 9*). If he has this objective attitude toward his possessions, he is well armed against life's hazards. One telling statement says, "He is not afraid of evil tidings" (*v. 7*). His success in life puzzles and exasperates the greedy man, who may have wealth, but who, as we might say nowadays, lets it give him a stomach ulcer (v. 10). The opposite, precisely, of this happy man is the rich man of Luke 12:13–21, who lays up useless treasure but has no treasure "toward God." Skeptics who feel uncomfortable about the cheerful liberality of this psalm should remember, (1) that there was no question, in Hebrew teaching, of any reward elsewhere than in this life, and (2) that the passage in Luke, ch. 12, not any superstitious notion of rewards "in the sky," is the real completion of this teaching about generosity.

Even so, there is one enormous question left outstanding by these meditations on human goodness. It is the question Bildad puts to Job (Job 25:4): "How then can man be righteous before God?" Before the God of whom the psalms speak no less eloquently than Job, how can such a wayward creature as man, so self-deceiving and unreliable in conscience, measure up to anything resembling the righteousness required by the Lord?

Paul's answer is, simply, justification by faith (Rom. 5:8), but the psalmist came very near it in his lofty moments.

PSALM 143

We have already noticed the psalmist's special love for the precept of "silence." A quick look back at Ps. 131 furnishes a very attractive picture of it. But if a man is silent before God, he will hear God's rebuke and will begin to feel the virtue of "penitence" arising in him.

Psalm 143 is a characteristic psalm of penitence. (Seven psalms of penitence were recognized by the medieval church: Ps. 6, 38, 51, 86, 102, 130, and 143.) It is the work of a man in the familiar position of being under pressure from a world that does not acknowledge his values. He begins his prayer with memorable words that echo those in Job:

> Enter not into judgment with thy servant;
>   for no man living is righteous before thee.

A man, you might say, may be as good as the man of Ps. 15 or Ps. 112, but before God he may still feel as far as ever from perfection. The singer goes on to make his urgent prayer. Life is almost too much for him (*vs. 3–4*), but he remembers all that he knows of God's historic goodness (*vs. 5–6;* cf. Ps. 77:11–20). After renewing his prayer to be delivered from the sense of futility and fatigue that the pressures have generated (*vs. 7–8*), he throws himself on the mercy and the wisdom of God:

> Teach me to do thy will,
>   for thou art my God!
> Let thy good spirit lead me
>   on a level path!
>   (*V. 10*)

This is penitence—silence before God. It needs no specialized knowledge of psychology to enable anyone to see that it is silence that brings mental relaxation and peace under pressure. And if the "adversaries" of *v. 12* are thought of as ulcer-generating anxieties and nightmares, then the proper treatment for them is to make oneself a channel for the power of God, which is life to all goodness and death to such "adversaries" as these.

This juxtaposition of complaint about life's pressures and silence before God who will "teach" the way of peace is often to be found in psalms of penitence. Psalm 5, for example, which is largely given to picturesque imprecations on the "enemies," says:

> Lead me, O LORD, in thy righteousness
>   because of my enemies;
>   make thy way straight before me.
> (Ps. 5:8)

In Ps. 25 we have the same thought: "Let not my enemies exult over me. . . . Make me to know thy ways. . . ." (Ps. 25:4). In Ps. 86, a psalm of larger compass, which contains a magnificent passage calling on God to show his righteousness to all the nations (Ps. 86:8–10), there is the same idea:

> Teach me thy way, O LORD,
>   that I may walk in thy truth.
> (Ps. 86:11)

And, of course, Ps. 119 is constantly placing the peace of obedience over against the trouble that life brings to the believer.

PSALM 51

But all of this is really leading toward the highest moral peak in the Psalter, *Ps. 51*. This psalm has a special historical note in its heading, to the effect that it was sung by David after Nathan had convicted him of his appalling offense in the matter of Bathsheba, the wife of Uriah the Hittite (II Sam., ch. 12). On this we may comment only that this tradition was the highest compliment that later Jews paid to David; if they thought he could, after such a rebuke, rise to this, then indeed they had confidence in him!

However that may be, *Ps. 51* is an unparalleled document of spiritual therapy. Nobody who allows it to enter into his heart can but be healed by it.

Here is a man who has already undergone moral surgery; his "sin" is exposed, and now he asks that it may be "blotted out," which means erased, made as though it had never been (*vs. 1–2*). What he has come to see (and what any sinner needs to see) is that his sin is not merely an error, or a mistake, or an offense against society. It is an offense against the Author of the universe and of all goodness. "Against thee, thee only . . ." Sin looks blackest when it is seen in its real context, which is a universe ordered by a loving and forgiving God. If palpable consequences came of it, they were no more than a just reward. The psalmist feels as though he is swallowed up in sin, made of nothing but sin. (*Vs. 4–5*.) (*Verse 5*, by the way, should not be taken too subjectively. It can be said that "total depravity" does not mean that man made in God's image is incapable of any good; it means that he is never immune from the forces that spoil goodness.)

He feels dirty, and needs washing. He searches passionately for innocence and cleanness. (*Vs. 6–12;* cf. Ps. 26:6.) In the end he will be able again to worship (*v. 15*), to be as those who may come to the "holy hill" (Ps. 15:1; 24:3). And when he comes he will know that the outward forms of worship are transformed when the heart has been worn down (the real meaning of "contrite," *v. 17*) by the love of God.

Verses 18 and *19* were added to the psalm to make it possible for congregational use. Their disconcerting reference to bulls and burnt offerings offends many modern readers. They need not. For personal devotion, and indeed for Christian worship, *vs. 1–17* are enough. For the ancient Israelite, there was a case for saying that it would not be quite right to describe the only way of outward worship he knew (the sacrifice of something valuable to himself) as the merest nonsense. To do so might easily undermine the confidence of a man who had not got so far as the exalted condition of mind described in the rest of the psalm—it might even prevent his getting there.

But primarily, this is the greatest of the psalms of silence, the most contemporary and the most original of all the psalms in the whole book.

Indeed, it brings us to what may be our epilogue. In connection with Ps. 96 (Chapter 6) we mentioned a beautiful but quite spurious reading that applied the psalm to the passion of Christ. There was one other beautiful "deliberate mistake" in a certain manuscript of the Latin Psalter, in the opening of Ps. 65. The true Latin text was *te decet laus*—"Praise is due to thee." One scribe wrote *tibi silet laus*—"Praise is silent before thee." Praise and silence—those are the two doctrines that the psalmists contribute to Israel's treasury of faith. And like that other variant in Ps. 96, this one in

Ps. 65 also found its way into a great hymn, with which we close:

> God is in heaven, and men below;
> Be short our tunes, our words be few;
> A sacred reverence checks our songs,
> And praise sits silent on our tongues.
>
> —*Isaac Watts*

EPILOGUE

On Using the Psalms in Worship

Now that we have begun to understand the psalms, what shall we do with them? We can, of course, read them privately, and it is assumed that we have been doing that. But what use can be made of them in worship? In order to encourage greater use of the psalms in the congregation, I am proposing a number of techniques and a few reflections on liturgical considerations.

First, there are several possible techniques for the use of the psalms in congregational worship.

a. The easiest way to use the psalms is to read them communally, either responsively or in unison. Certain hymnals provide selections arranged for this purpose. This is better than nothing, but it has very little aesthetic appeal, and the sound that results usually does scanty justice to the rhythm, the drama, or the profundity of the text.

b. Dramatic reading is a possibility which should be explored in using many of the psalms. Different parts can be assigned to different voices, or to a single voice alternating with the whole company in unison for a refrain. Psalm 91, for example, is assignable to three voices; Ps. 24, to several groups.

c. The easiest musical way for Protestant congregations to use the psalms is to sing them metrically, as the Scots do. Presbyterians in the United States have the psalms in a less archaic and awkward version than that in traditional use in Scotland. The tunes are always easy, and usually the words of the Psalter are faithfully followed. Certain hymns (such as "Our God, Our Help in Ages Past") that keep close to the words and thought of the psalms can be used to the same purpose. The disadvantage of this method is that it is never practicable to sing the whole of any but the shortest psalms. One has to be content with a small section of a psalm, thus losing the movement of thought in the original.

d. The easiest method for those not inhibited by Protestant prejudice is undoubtedly plainsong, using the Gregorian tones. These are always simple—hardly more than stylized speech. A good musician at the organ can make the accompaniment very beautiful in a modest way. Since these accompaniments are never written out and must always be improvised, it is necessary for the musician to know the rules and the opportunities of the modal scheme that governs these settings. If plainsong is used, it should always be antiphonal—one verse for the congregation, one for the choir—with the opening half verse sung by a soloist and responded to by the whole congregation. A pointed Psalter is required, of which the most serviceable is Briggs and Frere's *Manual of Plainsong for Divine Service*, ed. by J. H. Arnold (Novello, 1952).

e. A development of plainsong is the "Anglican

chant," familiar to many. Here the Biblical or the Prayer Book text can be sung in its entirety. There is a difficulty, however, when it comes to congregational performance. These tunes, often in sophisticated musical forms and always in four-part harmony, cannot help rousing a conflict between the rhythmic implications of the music and the rhythm of the words. Ideally these should be sung by a choir and listened to by the congregation. The choir can then achieve a rhythmic freedom and subtlety that a congregation cannot usually manage. The music provides a valuable interpretation of the words if it is well chosen. But for a congregation some familiar psalms go quite well with Anglican chants and no great harm is done if they are sung with a certain rough-hewn rhythmic obstinacy.

f. A more recent development is the use of antiphonal psalmody in the style usually associated with the name of Joseph Gelineau, the French priest-musician who introduced it to the church in 1953. Here a choir or a soloist sings the narrative of the psalm while the congregation at certain indicated points (sometimes after each verse) responds with a refrain set to simple rhythmical music. In Gelineau's own system this is a carefully systematized musical form, using the same modes that were used for plainsong. Among those who have now adapted the style to other musical idioms are Lucien Deiss, for example, and in England, Peter Tranchell, William Tamblyn, and Stephen Dean. Examples can be found in *New Songs for the Church, Book I* (Galaxy) and in *Praise the Lord* (Chapman, 1972). The Canadian *Catholic Book of Worship* (1972) has some other interesting examples, and several recent Catholic hymnals produced in the United States have experimented in new antiphonal styles. It should be observed that very lengthy psalms cannot readily be sung to this style simply because the antiphons and the new translations tend to make a psalm adapted to this style much longer than the original text. But for psalms of fifteen or even twenty verses the style is admirable and musically as satisfying as anything except plainsong.

g. Choral. Many choral pieces use the words of the psalms, and these can be chosen as anthems to be sung by a choir. But this choice should be subject to the liturgical considerations set out below.

Second, there are certain liturgical considerations relating to the use of the psalms in public worship. People are often more confused about liturgical matters than they are about techniques. Broadly speaking, there are two ways in which the psalms can be used in public worship. One is to use very short psalms or sections of psalms in the manner in which they are prescribed (though too infrequently sung) for the Mass or the Eucharist. This uses the thought of the psalm to direct the congregation's attention to some special point relevant to that day's liturgy. (The observation made in Chapter 2 about Ps. 139 and Easter Day is an example of such use.) The other is to treat the psalms as musical readings, and to associate them with the Scripture lessons in the service. The best place for a psalm so treated (in which case of course one would expect to sing a whole psalm, and therefore, ideally, to use techniques *c* or *d* above) is before or after the Old Testament reading. Once the service has progressed into the New Testament a psalm is not really relevant, and a

Christian canticle or hymn should be sung.

If you are confined to metrical psalms or to hymns that are psalm paraphrases, the same principle should apply. And it should also apply if the choral contribution to the service is set to a psalm text, or to any Old Testament text. Whereas the former way of using the psalms must be congregational to make its full effect, this way of using them need no more be congregational than the Old Testament reading. Sometimes a psalm will communicate if it is read communally: but another psalm will make its message clearer if it is sung to the congregation, as presumably most of the psalms originally were. Perhaps all can sing Ps. 46 very effectively; but Ps. 40 will almost certainly make its point better if it is sung by a soloist or a choir and the people attend to it without joining in.

And of course, as with technique *b* above, the occasional dramatic use of choir, solo, and congregation to represent the different levels of communication in the text will often be most welcome. With a minimum of rehearsal and stage management, it is easy to do.

Whatever the possibilities, the thing to remember is that these songs are wise, passionate, crude and human. There is no need to make them sound pious, although communal speech or song always requires some form of restraint and discipline. What has been said in our expository notes is enough, I think, to indicate how raw, and yet how humane, these songs are. Whatever music can do to enhance their grandeur and their tenderness should be offered to the worship of the church.

INDEX OF PSALMS

This index shows in which chapter of this book a psalm is dealt with. A reference in parentheses indicates passing mention.

Psalm	Chapter	Psalm	Chapter
1	13	33	4
2	8, (13)	34	(3)
4	11	37	(3), 12
5	(13)	38	(13)
8	8	39	12
10	(3)	40	1, (3)
11	11	41	(1)
13	11	42	5
15	13	43	5
16	3	44	3
19	10	46	(1), 9
22	1, (2), (10)	47	8
23	8	48	9
24a	13	49	12
24b	8	50	3
25	(3), (13)	51	13
26	13	53	(3)
27	8	54	1
28	(7)	55	11
29	7, (9)	57	3
30	4	62	11
31	(1), (4)	65	7, (13)
32	4	66	4

Psalm	Chapter	Psalm	Chapter
67	7	113	2
68	9, (11)	114	2
69	1	115	2
72	6, (9)	116	2
73	(3), 12	117	2
77	10, (11), (12), (13)	118	2
		119	(3), 10, (13)
78	(3), (9)	120	5
80	11	121	5
81	3, (10)	122	5, (7)
82	10	123	5
84	5	124	5, (3)
86	(13)	125	5
87	9	126	5
88	(1)	127	5, (13)
90	10, (12)	128	5, (13)
91	10	129	5
93	6, (7)	130	5, (13)
95	10	131	5, (13)
96	6, (7)	132	5, (6)
97	6, (8)	133	5
98	6	134	5
99	(1), 6	136	(1), (2), (12)
100	6	137	11
101	6	139	2
102	(13)	141	11
103	(3), 4	143	13
104	7, (9)	144	6
105	(3), (6)	145	(3), 9
106	(3)	146	4, (9)
107	12	147	7, (9)
110	8	148	7, (9)
111	3	149	(9)
112	13	150	9